**Judy McKay** has spent the last 20 years working in the high tech industry with particular focus on software quality assurance. She has managed departments encompassing all aspects of the software lifecycle including requirements design and analysis, software development, database design, software quality assurance, software testing, technical support, professional services, configuration management, technical publications and software licensing. Her career has spanned across commercial software companies, aerospace, foreign-owned R&D, networking and various Internet companies.

Judy has been conducting training seminars nationwide for seven years. Her informative courses are based on the real world application of practical data. Her courses cover the spectrum of software quality assurance, including creating and maintaining a world class quality assurance team, designing and implementing quality assurance and effective testing, and creating and implementing useful test documentation and metrics.

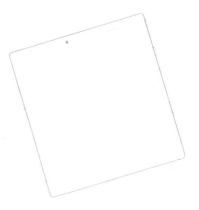

Judy McKay

Managing
the Test People

A Guide to Practical Technical Management

rockynook

Editor: Jimi DeRouen
Copyeditor: Nathan Schneider
Layout and Type: Josef Hegele
Cover Design: Helmut Kraus, www.exclam.de
Printer: Friesens Corporation, Altona
Printed in Canada

ISBN 978-1-933952-12-3

1st Edition
© 2007 by Rocky Nook Inc.
26 West Mission Street Ste 3
Santa Barbara, CA 93101

www.rockynook.com

Library of Congress catalog application submitted

Distributed by O'Reilly Media
1005 Gravenstein Highway North
Sebastopol, CA 95472

This book is printed on acid-free paper.

Preface

This book is written for managers, leads, and those who may soon find themselves in a technical leadership position. It focuses on some of the unique problems in the software quality assurance profession, yet the bulk of the book is generally applicable to any technical management job. It provides practical advice for the novice and affirmation for the expert. It contains real world stories which illustrate the concepts discussed in the text.

My writing style is informal and this book is meant to be an easy, fast read. No one has much extra time and we all read enough technical material, so this is a short, practical book without a lot of elaboration and extra words. I like to get to the point, make it, and move on.

In dealing with the pronoun "he" or "she", I compromised on the rules of grammar and went with the plural "they" in some instances where "he" or "she" could have been used. I find it distracting to read a book that switches between "he" and "she", so by default I used "he" when "they" would have been awkward. I didn't do this to ignore the population of women in the workplace, rather just to make it a bit easier to read. Please forgive this grammatical liberty.

This book provides guidelines and handy rules for various management situations. As always, you will have to tailor the information to fit your environment and your style. I've tried to explain the context from which I am writing in the various scenarios that are discussed. I've also included examples of the mistakes I've made in my over 20 years of technical management experience – hoping that you can learn from them, as I did, without having to suffer as much of the pain. In this book I've tried to include all the things I wish I'd known when I was starting out, even though I probably wouldn't have believed a lot of it until I'd seen it. Managing is a tough job. Managing a technical group is even tougher. Add to this the political issues of managing a quality assurance group, and you've really got your hands full. Being a successful manager requires great resourcefulness, common sense, confidence, and humility. Some of these traits are innate; some must be learned. For what you already know but need to reinforce, and for what you still need to learn to be successful, I hope this book helps.

Judy McKay
February 2007

Introduction

Ah, management ... a management position seems like such a good idea, doesn't it? You'll be great at it, you'll be the best manager ever, and you deserve the position. You've put in your time and you're ready for this substantial career move. But are you really ready? Do you understand what it takes to be a good manager, technical lead, or director? Most of us don't. Sure, we've seen lots of people fail, and we've seen the mysterious few who certainly should have failed due to their incredible lack of management skills, yet have successfully remained in positions of authority. Lets face it, if you are reading this book, you have the desire to be a good manager. A good manager is the kind of manager people will happily work for and with – the kind of manager you yourself want to have.

Management is not easy and it requires a different skill set than the one required for success in a technical position. In addition to the challenge of management in general, you want to manage a testing or quality assurance group. Now, you have really complicated your life! Many experts will tell you that like skills are required for managing people in any field because people are, after all, people. I agree that the majority of peoples' skills are applicable to any industry; however, managing in a technical field requires additional skills, and managing in a testing organization requires yet another set of skills in addition to the technical ones.

In this book, I'll discuss what it takes to be a successful manager in a technical environment, with some particular emphasis on managing a testing team. We'll walk through the life cycle of employment, from the recruiting and hiring processes all the way to terminations. Along the way, you will learn how to build that precious team, and how to keep it together for the long run.

Table of Contents

Table of Figures

1 The Perfect Beast

Before we get started on building our world-class testing organization, or, as I like to call it, "the perfect beast," we need to understand some of the necessary characteristics of a testing organization. While not every individual on your team has to have every characteristic, the more desirable characteristics which they have, the more flexibility you can extend in placing them in various positions on projects.

Staying with the beastly theme, what are we looking for? What qualities do our testers and quality assurance (QA) folks require that will allow us to build an elusive, perfect beast? The following traits would be great:

The brains of the finest development organization …

As a manager, it is our job to think of the things our team may have missed. As we carry out requirements reviews, code reviews, and the actual testing work, we must find the mistakes made by the developer or designer. That means our job is to outsmart them. We may be able to do this since we have a different focus; we approach the software from the customer's viewpoint, or maybe we are just more clever. It doesn't really matter how we do it, we just have to be able to do it. If testing never discovers a bug that the developer did not know about, what is the point of testing? If flaws are never found in the requirements design, did the review pay for itself? No. There is a reason why we test, and a reason why we review documents – it's because we find stuff they didn't.

It is a commonly held belief within development organizations that people are testers because they can't do development. From my experience, the best testers are capable of doing development, and in fact, some had been developers at a point in their careers. The good testers *choose* not to do development. They choose the interaction and the overall view that is afforded from the QA perspective. They want to have a positive influence on the customer's experience with the software. They want to ferret out the bugs that were put in the code by design or implementation errors. QA people have a different perspective. That doesn't mean they are not as capable or as technical as their developer counterparts; quite the contrary. It is this different perspective that makes them valuable to the organization; it is this special talent which they bring to the testing lab.

The enthusiasm of a wagging tail …

When the software is crashing, the build won't work, and the deadline is getting closer and closer, it can be hard to remain enthusiastic about the project. It is easy to be beaten down, discouraged, and to give up. But that is not what the perfect beast does. The perfect beast is excited by the prospect of a tight deadline and recognizes that now, more than ever, the focus is on the testing team's contribution to the project. This is what all the planning was for. This is when all eyes are on the test management to see if they really know where the project stands. This is the time to bring out all the metrics you've been creating throughout the project. This is the time to shine; so, as long as you did your planning, there is good reason to be enthusiastic.

The sharp eyes of an eagle …

Some of the smallest graphical user interface (GUI) problems can be the most annoying for the end user. It can be very difficult to be observant and pay attention to these details, particularly when you may be looking at the fiftieth release of the same software. But, this could be the time a typo is introduced that spells the name of your company incorrectly. It would be an easy typo to overlook, and a potentially catastrophic bug if released to the field. In my testing organizations, I've noticed that I am usually the least observant one in the group. I'll admit it's not a good trait, but it has certainly made me value those who have the special talent to remain consistently attentive. I have often found that the people who are the most observant are also the least technical. Why is that? It is partly because the technical people tend to look past the appearance of the software because they are busily analyzing its functions. This is one of the many reasons a department that is staffed with people of varied skill sets creates a stronger testing group – each individual has their strengths and weaknesses. As a manager, it is your job to utilize the strengths and mitigate the weaknesses. But, to do that effectively, you must recognize which is which.

The nose of a bloodhound …

When tracking down a problem, you may have to go through many layers in the software to trace its origin. Part of the job of the perfect beast is to follow that trail and to not get distracted on the way. Good troubleshooting is a precious skill that needs to be practiced and honed. The good news is that this can be easily learned from others on the job. I've spent many hours working with a developer as he traces through the software, trying different scenarios as he attempts to isolate a failure. The next time, I know what to do myself. From project to project the code will be different, but the same troubleshooting skills will always help you find your way to the ugly bugs. The same skills apply to design reviews and code walkthroughs. Persistence, knowing what to look for/ignore , and the ability to stay with the problem you're pursuing are critical to being a good bloodhound.

The bravery of a lion …

Have you ever had to walk into a meeting with your own managers to report that the much-revered schedule is now complete fiction? Do you have great empathy for gazelles on a lion-infested plain? Even if you have all your information together and can objectively present the data to the decision makers, it still takes a certain amount of guts to do it. You have to have the intestinal fortitude to do this job successfully. You also have to have the knowledge. We'll discuss some of the things you'll want to know along with some tricks that will help remove you from the prospective lion-chow list.

The skin of a rhinoceros …

Do the developers think you're unnaturally abusing their code? If they feel they are being unfairly targeted, you can expect the barbs to come flying in your direction. Even in the most amiable organizations, there are always a few points of contention, and those are likely to spawn some impatient grumbling. Don't let the little jibes bother you. Go after the cause of the contention, not the symptoms. The perfect beast lets the unkind comments roll off while addressing the root cause of the problem. People who are too thin-skinned and easily offended won't survive in the test environment when schedules are hot and people are hotter.

The empathy of a Labrador …

Someone has to take the side of the customer. Someone has to represent that customer's interests in the bug review meetings and in the approach to testing. That someone is often the test group – the last champion for the customer. Keep in mind that someday the software will be used by a real person, (or a real person will be writing code to interface with your software). Take care to empathize with that user; understand him, know what his needs are, and how he will use the software.

The indifference of a cat ...

Have you ever tried to make a cat feel guilty? Didn't work, did it? That is because cats don't care what you think about them. In the QA business, you have to do the right thing, even if it's not popular. If your best friend is in development and you are testing his code (which is causing the rest of the software to crash), it's your job to document the issues – even if it means you'll have to pay for his lunch for the next month. There is a high level of integrity required in a world-class testing group. No one should target an individual, but the smelly software has to be identified and fixed or the entire organization will suffer. It's best to do the right thing and be popular, but that isn't always possible. Be as objective as you can. At least you will be respected for your honesty.

The perfect beast ...

These are the main features required for our perfect (though odd-looking) beast. Every person you hire, every process you establish, and every representation you make of your group should reflect these characteristics. Combining them into a functioning whole can be a challenge. Not everyone on your team will have all the traits you seek, but you have to ensure that these are the predominant traits your team exhibits as a functioning unit.

Now that we know the characteristics of the beast, we're going to discuss:

How to Build the Perfect Beast
How to Make the Perfect Beast Effective
Leading the Perfect Beast
Evaluating the Perfect (or Not-So-Perfect) Beast
Feeding the Beast
Vaccinating (De-lousing) the Beast

2 How to Build the Perfect Beast

How did you get here? No, not how did you get to this chapter, but how did you get to this job?

Throughout this book, the term "manager" is used to identify any position that carries some personnel responsibilities. The responsibilities of someone with the title of "manager" may vary widely between companies, and could represent anything from a first line supervisor to a vice president. It really doesn't matter what the title is – if you are responsible for people, you are a manager.

There are three common ways by which you find yourself in a management position:

You were promoted from within
You inherited the department
You started the department yourself

Each of these has its unique challenges. Although every company is different, following are some general guidelines and practical advice drawn from a number of software and hardware development companies of varying sizes.

Promoted From Within

So, you've just returned triumphantly from your boss's office aglow with the knowledge that you have now achieved the vaunted position of manager. As you rearrange your office (or pack your cube to move to better accommodations) and think about how to position your chairs to receive your newly designated staff, what should be your first concern? How to dress tomorrow? How to stay awake during meetings? No. You should be thinking about how you are going to deal with the peer pressure your new position will bring to you.

What is peer pressure? Peer pressure is dealing with the expectations of your new and former peers. Peer pressure is very real, particularly in the work place. Ignoring it will certainly be an error and could lead to a disaster. Like it or not, everyone is watching you in your new job. They want to know what you will change, and how the promotion might change you. Your manager wants to see how you will handle your new responsibilities. Your former co-workers are wondering how you will handle your new authority. One of the best ways to deal with peer pressure positively is to interpret it as people having an honest interest in you. It's true; people are interested. This is a much more positive approach than to assume everyone is waiting to criticize you. Remember, if you are defensive, people will immediately assume you have a reason to be defensive.

New Responsibilities

One of the most difficult parts of any new job is to determine the expectations your manager has for you. I have had a number of occasions during my career to promote people into their first management position. When I promote someone, I have expectations for their performance in that new job, some of which I tell them clearly and some of which I assume they know. I don't expect a new supervisor to know how to do performance reviews, where to find the forms, or which meetings to attend. I do expect a new supervisor to know to talk and listen to their people, and to try to understand their people. Now that I'm older and wiser, I also know that this is not necessarily a realistic expectation.

So let's assume that your manager has particular expectations for you. How do you figure out what those are? Ask! Sit down and have a detailed discussion with your manager regarding exactly how he sees you fitting into your role. Remember, you have responsibilities that go upward – to your manager – and downward – to your people. You are no longer just responsible for yourself. You might at first be tempted to worry about how you will perform your job and about what your duties are, but this reflects only the concerns of your manager. Now, the people who work for you represent a whole new set of responsibilities.

Talk with your manager about his expectations for you in this role. Ask questions. Ask for advice. Consider informing him that you don't really know how to do this new job, and you need help from a mentor. As a manager, I appreciate when people under me ask to have my expectations clarified. Not only does it allow me to clearly communicate what I want, it also makes me really think about what I'm expecting. You have to remember, when your manager promotes you, he's been thinking about it for some time. While you might have thought it was coming, you probably didn't visualize yourself in the role until actually receiving the promotion.

Remind Us to Remember

As I look back, each time I have promoted someone to a supervisory position, it has been after considerable thought. By the time I do the paperwork and deliver the good news, I've had that person in my mind (for a particular role) for a month or two. Honestly, I expect them to just step in and do the job. I have a new and much more realistic view of what it takes to make the move when an employee sits down with me, notating my explanations and expectations. It's probably been awhile since your manager made a similar transition. It has been for me. Sometimes, you have to remind us to remember what it was like.

Here's a way to begin. You need to know how long your manager is expecting you to be in the learning phase of your new job. It's time to sit down with him and set out a timeline which you both can agree to; one you honestly feel you can meet. Once again, it's up to you to remind your manager that you will require a learning phase. Remember, he probably expects you to move into your position and naturally know what to do. Though unrealistic, it is often true, so deal with it professionally and turn it to your advantage. Your manager has created a learning opportunity for you, and is the best candidate to serve as your teacher. Get him to commit to helping. Now, your success is tied to his success in a visible way.

Bob Wants a Plan

Will you still have technical responsibilities in your new role? Probably. This is the time to sit down with your manager and clarify exactly what his expectations are for your technical contribution. Let's look at a likely scenario. You bravely approach your manager to ask who should take over your technical work. You've now earned lion points for being brave and for airing the problem. Unfortunately, you've also committed one of the big mistakes – you've brought a problem to your manager without proposing a solution. You'll soon learn this lesson from the other side of the desk – you don't want people to just bring you problems; you want them to bring you possible solutions as well. If someone comes to you with both a problem and solution, you know they have thought about it and put some effort into solving the problem. This is the person you begin to value because they're working with you. The person who only brings you problems soon becomes an unwelcome guest; though you must tolerate them.

What is the most likely answer when you walk into your manager's office and say, "So Bob, who should take over my technical work now that I have all this important manager stuff to do?" You're likely to get one of two responses. "I don't know. It's your group now, you figure out how to handle the extra work." Bob then quickly returns to shuffling his papers, hoping that you'll get the hint, leave, and solve the problem yourself. Secondly, he could also answer, "Well, I promoted you because I thought you were ready for the job. Unfortunately, we can't increase the headcount right now so you're going to have to figure out how to partition out your work within your group." Then Bob looks at you expectantly, hoping you brought a proposal with you. Either way, it should be clear to you that this is your problem to solve. The important thing at this point, is to come back with a plan and present it to Bob. This will accomplish two things. First, you will show that you can work up a solution for a problem, and that you can work with him to get advice and suggestions. Secondly, you will have a chance to lay out (in detail) just how much work there is to be done. When you leave this meeting, Bob should have the good impression that you can deal with a problem, as well as a more realistic understanding of what the workload is.

Will Success Change You?

Your former peers expect you to stay the same. Let's face it, that's just not practical. The expectation is there though, so you need to deal with it. How will you handle this new relationship in a positive way?

First of all, think about how you like to be managed. Do you like every detail of what you need to do micromanaged? Do you like to be given directions without being given the chance to add your opinion? Probably not. If you do, you don't belong in management – you should probably return this book before you spill coffee on it. So, assuming you prefer to have some flexibility when you are given your directions, it is safe to assume your people will want the same from you. Now you have to determine how much autonomy you can give your people, while still feeling comfortable that you have control over the deliverables for which you are accountable. That's right – it's harder than it seems. Giving up control requires trust, but trust should be earned. Unfortunately, the trust can't be earned unless the opportunity is given. So get ready to chew off your nails, because you're going to have to give up some control in order to get your team working independently and efficiently.

Benevolent Ruler or Evil Tyrant? (How Do You See Yourself?)

Maybe, the better question is, how will people see you? We're back to the peer pressure issue. There is almost always someone who will feel a certain amount of jealousy toward you. They will ask why you were promoted and not them? These are difficult issues to deal with, and with luck, your manager will be aware of the potential for problems and will have made it very clear to your peers why you were chosen when the promotion was announced; or maybe not. Either way, be aware that not all your followers will be loyal or even willing. Now it's your job to win them over – to bring them onto your team.

Never underestimate the scrutiny you will now be under. As soon as you go to lunch with one of your team members, others on the team will wonder why they didn't get to go. What did you talk about? Did you talk about other team members? Why did you select to go with that person? That's right, even an innocent lunch may now become a blossoming mushroom of discontent in the department. Many people feel insecure. In fact, their insecurity is generally not related to their technical knowledge, but with their social interactions. If you walk into their office and challenge them on a technical issue, you will receive a much better response than if they feel that you didn't want to go to lunch with them. Each individual is unique, so part of your new challenge is to figure out what makes each one tick – and to not offend anyone in the process.

But what about lunch?

I worked with a software development director who was truly brilliant – and really quite weird. He was great to work for, his designs were excellent, and he was a talented teacher. Unfortunately, he was the most avoided lunch companion in the company. This worked out well most of the time because he didn't really want to go to lunch with us either. Once a year though, he felt the need to take employees to lunch on their employment anniversary. Oh, how we dreaded that lunch. We'd make outlandish excuses to get out of the "stare at your plate" lunch. We didn't want to hurt his feelings by telling him we rated lunch with him right up there with going to the Department of Motor Vehicles without an appointment – in fact, the Department of Motor Vehicles trip had the edge.

Finally, one courageous individual suggested that rather than his taking us out individually throughout the year, we'd rather take him out as a group on his anniversary date. He readily accepted this and admitted that he hadn't really liked the individual lunches, but *his* manager had told him he needed to have more individual interaction with us. We promised to meet with him anytime we had a problem (which we already were doing) and he promised to do away with the lunches. It was a happy solution all around, but it did require some honesty. The lesson here is to remember that you are now the manager with the power to command people to be your lunch date. Use it carefully. It's hard to turn down a lunch date with the boss. If you don't mean it to be a business meeting, be sure they understand there's no obligation.

In addition to your awesome power to command lunch dates, you now have some level of control over people's jobs and careers. Don't let this go to your head! When you sit back in your new office, put your feet on your desk and wait for your subjects to enter, bow, and grovel before you, STOP. You need to rethink this. You are not the all powerful tyrant. This is not your time to exact revenge upon those who made it hard for you to get where you are. This is the time you should be aware of the gravity of the tasks before you. You are no longer leading projects – you are leading people. People have lives. When they go home and someone asks them, "So, how's the new boss?" they are talking about you! Be sure they have positive things to say.

I Can't Really Tell You This, But …

As you move up in a company, you have access to more information. Sometimes you have access to more information than you want to have. I worked for a company that decided they would be doing a layoff after the first of the new year . They told me about it in October. Through November and December we worked on the percentages to be laid off and the total headcount effect. I remember sitting in my office on the evening of the company Christmas party making the final layoff list. One of my people stopped by work on his way to the party to introduce me to his wife.

They were all dressed up and excited to be going to what was guaranteed to be a really nice evening. I had just added his name to the list. It was the correct decision in order to meet the company goals and it had been a hard one to make, but clearly he belonged on the list. I felt rotten.

So sometimes you know what you might wish you didn't. And sometimes you know exciting things that you can't share. Anytime you are told something that you would like to share with your staff, be sure to ask if you can share it. It can be hard to tell, and it is always safer to check first. On the flip side, your people are going to expect you to share everything you know. Chances are, you can't. What they need to understand is that you will share with them everything you know that is appropriate to be shared. Be careful how you present this. If you say, "You can count on me to tell you everything you need to know," there's the implication that they aren't important enough to know about all the cool stuff. It sounds much better to say, "I'll promptly share with you everything I've been told, unless I've been told I can't". And, it sounds better yet if you can give an explanation. For example, "I can't give you the quarter closing numbers until they have been announced to the public because of SEC rulings." People know you'll have information they won't have. They just need the assurance that you'll tell them the important parts as soon as you can.

But, how do you gain this trust? By earning it. We've all been told about a management open door policy, only to see the doors slam shut and the shades go down as soon as the stock drops. Yet, this is the time people need the most reassurance. Tell them what you can, even though it may not be complete. And, tell them there are things you're not allowed to tell them. Be honest. Talking about the issue instead of avoiding it or hiding in the restroom will help calm the masses. Frequently, I have had people from other departments ask me what's going on. And I tell them all I can.

An empathetic dog can be a manager's best friend. You can tell them anything and they will reliably keep your secrets

Inheriting the Department

Inheriting an existing department by being hired from outside the company is a completely different scenario from being promoted from within. Now you're the outsider. You are also the one chosen by management and most likely an unknown. So, what are you going to do on the first day to prevent yourself from destroying your opportunities?

Making the First Impression

Remember dating? Well, this is worse because no matter how well you do, you're unlikely to get taken out to dinner and kissed goodnight. (If that happens you might want to reconsider this position!) First impressions do matter. Your people are likely to be nervous, resentful, accepting, or a combination of these feelings. Remember how you felt the last time you got a new manager? Those are all natural feelings, and you should expect to be met with a mix of responses. I took a job as a QA Director in a company that had two QA divisions. One had been without a manager for about six months. They were thrilled I was coming on board to provide some guidance and control over the schedules that had become unreasonable. The other division was not at all pleased to see me, and felt that one of the existing managers should have been promoted to my position. That's a very difficult situation to overcome. For my own peace of mind, I spent some time investigating why he hadn't been promoted. It didn't take long to discover that he didn't have enough respect in the development organization to be successful in that role. However, he did not recognize this shortcoming, and was very resentful of me before he even met me. It was an uphill climb for a long time. I had to work with him, continually asking for his input, asking him for past history, and working to get him on my side. In the process, I also had to prove to him that I was qualified for the job; in fact, more qualified than he was.

While you don't want to be touting how great you are, you do need to make it clear to your new department that you are qualified to lead them, and that you've been successful doing so elsewhere (even if only at a project level). Part of making a good impression is to sell yourself a little. Call the group together so they all hear the same information simultaneously. Introduce yourself. Explain your qualifications. Tell them you'll be meeting with them individually to talk about what they do and what they want to do. Keep it short and be positive. You're glad to be in this new job and you're going to make it work with their help. Generally, people want to like their manager. That works to your advantage. Most people will approach a new manager with the hope that it will be a positive relationship.

But Why Are You Really Here?

Now for the tricky part. You were brought into this position for a reason. What is it? Oh sure, you were told something politically correct during the interview, but unless you received some really honest information, you can bet there's information you need regarding why you are really here. It's time to find out! Sit down with your manager and your team and find out what you are replacing or changing or starting, and why. Were there mistakes that were made in the past that you don't want to repeat? I once came into a position where the previous manager had offended the technical leader of the development group. During my interview, the development manager said that the entire QA group should be fired – they were all incompetent. Oh good. I could see I had my work cut out for me. It did take me a couple weeks to find the root of the resentment. Once I found the bridges that needed to be repaired, it actually wasn't hard to fix them. The trick is figuring out where the current problems are and where the past problems were.

You need to ascertain who does what to whom, when and why

Each organization is different. Different departments within the same company can vary widely. As quickly as possible, you need to ascertain who does what to whom, when, and why. How does work normally flow? Is it working effectively? Remember, you need to understand what is currently being done and how effective it is before you try to make changes. You will be seen as a brilliant leader if you ask people for their input. Soon you'll be seen as quite perceptive when you start to champion their causes. Remember, early successes are very important. Go after a couple little nagging problems that you can easily fix. I started at one company where they were having daily bug status meetings. My people hated those meetings, and for some reason, the practice was for the whole department to go (security in numbers?). I told them that if they could get me up to speed on all the open bugs, I'd go to all the meetings and they wouldn't have to. You should have seen the concentrated effort that was applied to educate me on those bugs. Along the way, I learned a lot about the product and about the quality of my people. My people were thrilled that I had delivered them from the dreaded meetings. They were also surprised by how quickly I learned the product. They forgot they had been the ones teaching me, because they were concentrating on telling me about the bugs. And, by the way, I got the meetings changed to weekly instead of daily.

Understand before you change

Supporters and Adversaries

Remember, you have to sort out your supporters and your adversaries. You may have only supporters. Great! This will be easy. Somewhere in the organization, you can almost bet you'll have an adversary – someone who will thwart your efforts and do some undermining. You need to find these folks and win them over. Understand their motives. Do they resent you because they wanted a friend to be hired instead of you? Do they think they should have had your job? Do they fear that you will monitor their hours and find they actually only work from 10-2 each day?

While you're mired down in your internal issues, remember, your management brought you into this job for a reason. Do you know what your goals are? If not, find out. Now is the time to sit down with your boss and see what his one-month, two-month, three-month, six-month, and one-year goals are. This will help you mold your goals to match his. And remember; be prepared to go into this meeting with some observations and questions of your own. It will make you look like you're interested in the job, and that you've hit the ground running. You don't have to ask profound questions; just logical ones which show you know your stuff. For example, "I've normally worked with a system of daily builds. I notice that we are getting weekly builds, but I understand the developers are doing daily builds. Is there a reason why QA only takes builds once a week?" This shows you've looked into the build system, and that you're bringing some experience to the table. You're asking why, instead of rushing ahead and implementing a system you've used before, which might not be applicable to this environment.

Evaluate Your Staff

Find the good, bad, and indifferent

Take a deep breath … This is where you find out what you've gotten yourself into. It's time to talk to each person in the group and figure out what you've got. I try to set aside an hour for each person for this first meeting. In my experience, most people won't take that long, but if they know they have a dedicated hour of your time, they will be relaxed and feel that they have adequate time to talk about whatever is on their mind. Depending on the size of the department, you may not be able to get to everyone in the first week. If you can't, be sure to make appointments for everyone so they know they will get their turn. If it's a tiny department, or if you want a more informal environment, you might want to take each person out to lunch.

(Be sure you're not the dreaded lunch date mentioned above though.) I like to give my staff members a choice. "I can meet with you tomorrow at 3:30 or we could go to lunch tomorrow, whichever works better for you." I've given them an easy way to get out of having lunch with me, but I also made it clear that I want to talk to them in whichever environment they prefer. In one of my recent jobs, each person opted for lunch – and that was fortunate for me because I'm always hungry and because they were all a little shy, so it took some time to draw them out. Having lunch was an excellent opportunity to get to know each person in a more casual and relaxed setting.

Take notes when you talk to people. You'll use them later as a reference, and if you're like me, you can write yourself little reminders so you can remember who is who. One guy I talked to was wearing a Cubs hat. I asked if he was a fan, and he said that he certainly was, being from Chicago. From then on, I tried to make a point of asking him how the Cubs were doing (or the Bears or Bulls, depending on the season). Try to find a way to connect with each person. It gives you an easy way to approach them and allows them see your human side, and that you are more than just a manager.

After You've Formed Your Impressions

Now that you've had a chance to form your own impressions, talk to the existing managers or leads about the people. Take a few (or many) hours, a lot of caffeine, and a good reading light, and sit down and go through all the old reviews. Look at everyone's resume. Remember, when you're looking at old reviews you don't know who wrote it, so take it as input but not as the authoritative word.

Now you have all the data. It's time to sit back and watch and get to know these people in their work environment. It can be difficult, but try not to make any judgments yet, and certainly don't make any assignment or position changes. Use all the background information you've gathered to do an accurate appraisal of each person in their current position. Remember, you're building your department for the future. You'll probably want to make some changes, but be patient; you want to be sure you make the right changes. If you're getting pressure from your manager to make alterations, but you don't feel you have enough information to do it fairly, explain that to him. Your manager will respect you for it. If he doesn't, well, your resume is still current …

Who Are the Leaders?

Would your current leaders get trapped in a paper bag?

Part of evaluating the staff is determining the leaders. The "natural leaders" make the best project leads and managers. Others will look to them for instruction without being directed to do so. Those natural leaders are the ones you want to develop. They already have the grassroots support and natural ability. Find them. Develop them. Get them into the key positions where they can grow and the team can benefit from their skills.

What if the leaders are tending to lead people off cliffs? It's time for a little investigative work. Are the people willingly following? Are they a bunch of lemmings (small furry animals reputed to have a tendency to follow each other off a cliff)? If people are following, your leaders have some good skills and probably just require better guidance. If people are not following or, even worse, are ridiculing the leaders, you will need to step in. This problem is discussed in the section "A Good Leader Gone Bad."

This is also the time to look at how projects are normally allocated. Do people tend to work with the same developers as they move between projects? Is there a seniority system? It's important to understand the existing system before you make any assignments. Maybe they're on a kind of rotation system, e.g., switching between a maintenance project and then a new development project. If someone has been working on a boring maintenance project for the last year while drooling over the upcoming new technology project, you'd better be aware of this before you mistakenly assign them to another boring maintenance project (or even an exciting maintenance project).

It's easy to step on toes, and this is certainly the time to be walking lightly until you understand the ways things work. If you have an established department, there will be established expectations. You'll save yourself a lot of pain if you take the time now to figure them out.

Shiny White Knights

Food is an effective and politically correct bribe

Shiny, white knights tarnish very easily. You must act quickly to make a good impression. In my experience, you have about two weeks to make that impression. Once a good impression is set, it will carry you for several months (assuming you don't do something really awful), but you have to make a positive impression and make it early. Let's face it, sometimes you have to rent loyalty until you can earn it. So, bring in bagels on Fridays!

And remember, the impression you make is not just important within your department. And, it might follow you after you leave.

Realistically, you only have about a month to develop a staffing plan, including any changes you want to make to existing staff. You only have about three weeks to understand the generalities of the projects you will be managing. Each company is entrenched in its own language. While you're given a grace period to learn the new nomenclature, if you still refer to bugs by the name you used at your last company after three weeks in the new company, it's going to give your staff a bad impression of you. You have to use your grace time wisely; it ends all too soon.

Starting the Department Yourself

The main challenges with starting a new department usually lie in the area of staffing. Staffing is discussed in the next chapter. In addition to choosing the people who will work under you, you will need to set up some guidelines and rules.

Creating Procedures and Processes

This is not a book on the correct processes and procedures to have in place. If you want that, you'll need to read many books, then figure out what works best in your environment. For your position as a manager, there are a few important things to remember. Procedures are often a precarious subject. Too many and you choke on them; too few and there are no rules. You have to know your organization and implement the minimum procedures first – you can add others later. The worst case is to implement too many procedures, or the wrong ones – then all subsequent ones will be ignored. So, when you arrive on the scene with your precious book of procedures that worked well for you at your last job, put the book in a drawer. First, you have to learn what procedures this company already has in place. Then figure out if they work. If they work, add them to your book for later use. If not, look at what needs to be changed. Remember, a procedure may be generally accepted without necessarily being effective.

Are the current processes lifesavers or anchors?

I've been with companies where there was a formal requirements review process. There were lengthy meetings to discuss the requirements, what they should be, how they should be implemented, and what the market expected. Detailed requirements documents came from these meetings. The requirements were clear, easy to implement, and easy to test.

A formal requirements review process is great, right?

Good procedure, right? Wrong. These beautiful requirements were always delivered after the product had already been developed. So, not only were they useless, but they failed to reflect what was in the real product. And, sadly, we couldn't use them for the next version because the market was changing so fast that we usually leapfrogged the written requirements.

Part of setting up effective procedures and processes is to be sure there is an adequate communication system in place. How is information transferred between departments? Will you know what you need to know when you need to know it? It's great to have QA test the help text for the product. If the help text isn't implemented until the entire product development is complete, there is a much larger test effort than would have been necessary had the help flowed in with the features.

Determining "Enough"

One of a new manager's challenges is to set up "enough" procedures and policies to get the work done efficiently without bogging down the entire system. Tread lightly. It's much easier to add procedures than it is to remove ones you've tried to implement. Removing a procedure you championed makes you look indecisive. It is better to wait a little longer, and be sure that what you want to implement will meet your goals. It's always better to get informal acceptance of a procedure or process before you push for formal implementation. For example, if people are already giving you release notes and you just want to add a couple more items of data, that's going to be fairly easy to implement. If they've never written a release note for any code, you need to ease into the practice or be ready to fight hard. It's also easier to implement a procedure if people understand why it is needed. It's rarely sufficient to say, "Because, if we do this we'll be nearing SEI CMMI level 2." Does that matter to the individual developer? Probably not. But, people are likely to cooperate if you say, "Because if you tell me what you actually changed in the code, I can test it more quickly and get the results back to you in 24 hours without having to sit in your cubicle for an hour while you explain it to me."

3   Finding Parts for the Perfect Beast

I love and hate staffing. At this point in your career, you are no longer most valuable as an individual contributor. Remember this and take it to heart – *you no longer matter; only your people do.* Your contribution is to find and keep the best possible people. Creating your own team from scratch is ideal, but it's also a tremendous responsibility. A difficult employee will take at least 30% of your time from the time the problem is recognized until the time the problem is resolved. If your incorrigible mistake takes you 90 days to fire, that's about 30 days you have devoted just to the problem child. Do you have that time built into your schedule? And what if you have two problem people, or three?

30% of your time will be spent on a problem employee

Obviously, the only alternative here is to avoid the problem employee in the first place. In some cases, you inherit one and just have to deal with it. We'll discuss ways to handle these difficult situations effectively in later sections. But, if you get to do your own hiring, it's well worth the time to make sure you're not setting yourself up for trouble. In this section, we're going to cover how to write a good job description, how to screen resumes, and, most importantly, how to interview. I've been hiring people for over twenty years. I've hired hundreds. I've fired two. Of the two I fired, I hired one. Not a bad record! Following are some of the guidelines that have worked for me.

Write a Good Job Description

With the current plethora of job sites on the web, writing a good job description is becoming more and more important. No longer will your description be seen only by subscribers to the local paper. This description may be seen by thousands of possible candidates, and not just candidates for the job. Future CEOs may be looking at job listings to see the caliber of people being sought by your company. Your job description must be able to stand up to some scrutiny! This is your chance to hook the people you really want, and discourage those you don't. Think long and hard about what you really need and want in your candidates. Spending enough time on this step will also later save you from reading through piles of inappropriate resumes.

I once let a new human resources (HR) recruiter write a job description for me. I ended up with 350 resumes in response to the posting. As I started to read through the pile, I realized that the recruiter had left out my requirements which stated: "Years of experience and education." Of the 350 resumes, only five met my needs. I learned then to always write my own job descriptions, and to double-check them after they are posted. What? Double-check? Do I sound suspicious? Surely no one would introduce a typo into my carefully worded job description, but there it was in nice bold print in a widely circulated newspaper: "Must be able to work in a multi-asking environment." Perhaps a "multi-asking environment" is a more accurate term, but we were really looking for people with experience programming in a multi-tasking environment.

Let's Get to the Point

Diplomacy required! A good job description should be brief and high-level. You don't want to exclude good candidates who might have similar experience but not direct experience with your product. If you do have specific requirements, state them and emphasize that they are actually required. Remember, you are telling a lot about your company through the description of the job. I recently read a job posting that emphasized the need for experience in dealing diplomatically with development, sales, support, and technical publications. Interesting. Obviously they had some issues where someone was less than diplomatic. This could be because the QA manager didn't have the necessary tact, or it could be that there were some unreasonable people in that organization. Regardless, management realized this was an issue, or they wouldn't have made that specific note in the job description. I took that as a positive sign.

A good job description should contain the following: an industry-accepted job title, a short description of the job, technical requirements, education requirements, pluses (things you'd like to see), and general skill requirements. Let's walk through an example of a job description.

Job Title – *Quality Assurance Automation Engineer*

- This is labeled as a QA job, so we've made it clear to the casual browser that the job is not limited to testing, but also includes input into the overall quality of the product.
- It's an automation job, not a manual test job, so the candidate can reasonably assume that the majority of the job will deal with automation.
- It's an engineer position, not an analyst or test position. The candidate can expect to architect and write code.
- The title you use here may not be the same as the one used in HR.

Job Description – *Candidate will be responsible for designing, coding, and maintaining an automation test suite for a large document management application. Candidate will be an individual contributor in a team of 3–5 other senior people.*

- We've outlined the job, including that the work encompasses design and maintenance – it's a long-term commitment to a new project.
- We've explained that this is a senior position, but not a lead position.

Technical Requirements

- Candidate must have minimum three years experience developing and implementing test automation software
- Candidate must have minimum five years QA experience
- Candidate must have minimum one year development experience
  - These are specific minimum requirements, clearly explained for someone in the industry.

Education Requirements – *Candidate must have BS degree in a technical field or equivalent experience.*

- In most environments, the more experience a candidate has, the less a degree matters. In others, the degree is critical regardless of experience. In some environments the degree is critical regardless of the field in which it was earned. Evaluate your needs before you set this requirement.
- Remember, existing members of your department are likely to read this. If there are department members without degrees and now you decide to require a degree, are you sending a message? If there has been a

change in the requirements, be sure to talk to everyone before you post your ad, and explain that current department members have no cause for concern.

***Technical Pluses** – In addition to the above requirements, the candidate should have two years of technical support experience and should have been actively involved in at least one field installation. Candidates with BS or MS degree in Computer Science preferred.*

- ■ This section is used to tell candidates they will have an advantage competing for the job if they have these assets. Note the use of 'should' instead of 'must'.

***General Skills** – Candidate must possess excellent organizational skills and must have extraordinary attention to detail. Excellent verbal and written communication skills are required for this position.*

- ■ This is the section to throw in everything you want in the ideal candidate. Do you need public speaking ability? Someone who can catch for your softball team?

Love Those Cover Letters

Now that you have written that great job description, you have to sort through all the resumes that will come pouring in as a response. I love to get cover letters – I always read resumes with cover letters first. Cover letters can be very informative. A good cover letter should tell you that the applicant researched the company. Did he carefully read the job description and customize the cover letter accordingly? Can he write a coherent sentence/paragraph/letter? Does he at least have a friend who can write coherently? Does he have no friends? Does he proofread? Proofreading is a sign of professionalism. You can be certain that someone who doesn't proofread their cover letter and resume isn't going to proofread bug reports or test plans.

I have received several cover letters that were so well written that I interviewed the candidate even though their resume was not exactly what I was seeking. Each time, the best cover letter came from the best candidate. Maybe I got lucky, but it's certainly a practice I'll continue.

Reviewing the Resumes

Ho-hum! Time to read resumes. So, there you are with your bunny slippers and your double espresso, ready to tackle the pile. Is there a fast way to skim through resumes? Sure there is. Or at least there's a fast way to figure out which ones you want to read in more detail. I have four quick checks I perform on each resume.

1. Is the resume neat? If the candidate doesn't have time to format the resume nicely, then I don't have time to read it. For web resumes that are pure text, I always ask for a formatted version rather than wading through the unformatted text.
2. Is the resume well organized? Does it follow a logical order?
3. Does the resume have all the pertinent information? Job history, education, etc?
4. Does the stated objective match my job opening? I've had a number of resumes for QA positions that clearly state in the objective that the candidate is seeking a development job or a way to get into development. I treat these with caution. I don't want my department to become the stepping-stone to a "better" job. Unless I really need an experienced developer for a short period of time, I generally pass.

I'm always reluctant to turn away a resume due to the risk of passing up a gem. Before I put a resume in the reject pile, I give it one more test: do I care if my dog shreds this resume? I was once reading a huge stack of resumes in my backyard and I had the reject pile sitting on the chair next to me. My dog came bounding up on the deck, dropped his ball, grabbed the pile of resumes and took off. I didn't care. That was when I knew those really were the rejects.

Another use for your dog as a management tool

Assuming our candidate's resume passes the above checks, it is time to do a more serious reading. Start from the back of the resume. This gives you several important pieces of information: how has this person's career evolved? How did they get into QA in the first place? What was their education, and if it was non-technical, where did they make the change to work in a technical field?

If it is an interesting resume, start jotting down some interview questions now. You probably won't do the interview for another week or two, and at that time you'll just take a cursory glance at the resume. Make notes now to save yourself time later.

Does Education Matter?

Is an educational degree noted on the resume? If they took courses toward a degree but didn't finish it, note that for an interview question. Maybe the person has trouble completing tasks. If they have a degree, is it pertinent? Does that matter? I like to see a technical degree of some type, but one of the best QA people I ever had working for me had a fine arts degree. Business degrees and subject matter expertise can be more valuable in some cases than computer science degrees. It depends on the position and your company. Do they note their GPA? If not, and if they've been out of school less than five years, ask them during the interview. Did they work while attending school? If so, and if the GPA is good, they've proven they can multi-task.

Now to the meat of the resume: the employment history. It's time to look at the specifics of each job they've listed. Even if the job is not directly applicable to the one you're hiring for, you can find out a lot about the person by asking about their past jobs during the interview. When looking at the resume, you want to see if their job history is generally applicable to the experience you need in the position you're trying to fill. Don't be narrow-minded here. In the high tech industry, a good, experienced person can easily acquire knowledge of particular technologies. The more experience someone has, the faster they will learn. Try not to dismiss candidates just because they don't have a specific job skill. Look at general experience; look at how often they have changed jobs and acquired new job skills. If you have someone who's bright and willing to learn, you can teach them any specifics they may be lacking.

What Did You Do for Your Company?

Assuming the applicant's job experience meets your needs, plan your interview questions now. I want them to be able to tell me about each of their past employment experiences; to explain what the company did, the purpose of the product(s) they produced, and what the candidate's involvement was in the company/department/team. What role did they play? This question is applicable for an individual contributor as well as a manager. Everybody should know what their role is within their company.

Additionally, I want to know about their past projects. I want them to describe to me some of the projects they've worked on. The answers to these questions tell me a lot about the person's enthusiasm, realism, and their ability to work with others. I can now discuss the technical details of their jobs, which procedures worked, and which were lacking. From this discussion I can see if I have a candidate who sees a problem and works to solve it, or if I have someone who mires down in problems and grouses about them.

If you don't know what you contributed to your company, I probably don't need you in mine

And Why Did You Leave?

Now that I'm on the subject of their jobs, I can ask some of the more difficult questions during the interview. I want to know why the candidate left each job. Each job. This can slow down the interview process, but it's invaluable information. Does this person jump from job to job for money? Do they leave when things start to get tough? Do they consistently choose bad companies (should I be worried that they picked my company?)?

I also want to know what they liked and disliked about each job. Get them to really think about the jobs they've had. By finding out what they enjoy doing, as well as what they dislike doing, I can get a good feeling for how well they'll like the job I have to offer and if they'll fit into my environment. I also like to know how their team was structured at each job. This can be significant if they're comfortable in an organizational structure that my company can't provide. I once worked at an Internet startup company and interviewed someone from a large aerospace company. One of the things they liked most about their previous job was the structure and formal environment where schedules were predictable and the work could be planned months in advance. Clearly, this person would not be happy in an unpredictable, unstructured environment where no apparent rules were in place. Not only would they have been miserable in the position I was seeking to fill, they also wouldn't have been successful.

If you get honest answers to these questions, you'll be able to predict how this person will work with others and how they'll deal with tough situations. If this is somebody who has only worked in an environment with a strict fence between development and QA, while you have a highly integrated group, this person may bring an unsavory "us vs. them" mentality. Or, maybe they'll welcome the integration. Ask them.

But What Do You Really Want to Do?

So you really want to be a professional basketball player?

While still looking at the job history on the applicant's resume, I want to see how much time this person has spent on each job and what kind of title progression they've had between and within jobs. If the person has only been promoted when they changed jobs, you might want to examine that issue during the interview. In the interview, I also want to know which job was their favorite – and why. In keeping with that theme, what would their ideal job be? Is that something my job will give them? It's also a perfectly reasonable question to ask what the candidate is expecting from this job. If they've researched your company and your excellent job description, they should have a well-formed answer. This tells you if you have a sincere candidate who has really thought about the job, and how they would fit in your company.

If a resume has passed your scrutiny to this point and you have been able to ask the above interview questions, you should now know what's important to the individual and if your opening matches what they want. If they expect to be promoted every year with a 10% salary increase (I actually had someone tell me that in an interview), you may have an issue. If they are coming from a very formal environment and expect promotions based on time and grade, you may have an issue. Look for people who want challenges and who don't run away from adversity. On the other hand, you want a candidate who knows when to cut their losses. There's nothing wrong with having left a hopeless situation – it was the smart thing to do.

Overstating and Downright Lying

"Experts" rarely are

Some people will list skill sets on their resume, which make good material for planning interview questions. If the candidate rates himself an 'expert', find out if he is. Experts rarely identify themselves as such – they don't need to. If you don't have the technical knowledge to determine if you're being conned, you may need to bring in a technical interviewer. It's better to do the extra interview than to hire someone who is under-qualified for your job. Remember to hold the person to what is listed on their resume. It's a sign of basic honesty. You will need to be able to trust this person when they're working for you. If they lie on their resume, they may also lie on their test completion report.

And speaking of lying on resumes; it can be difficult to fire someone *Can you ever trust a liar?* for lying on their resume, but it is a lot easier to fire them for lying on their application. If your company has a policy that each candidate must fill out and sign an application, be sure you read the application and compare it to the resume. I've been amazed at how educational degrees and job experience may differ between a resume and the official application.

In summary, be sure to plan interview questions from the data on the resume, as well as using your own favorite interview questions. The resume should be the single most professional document an individual will ever produce. Their test plans are not going to look any better! The resume is your first detailed look at a candidate; make efficient use of your time and read it carefully using the guidelines above. Look for the pertinent information. It should take you about one minute to look through a resume to determine if you want to read it more closely. That means you can shuffle through a pile of 60 resumes in one hour (assuming you have the mental stamina!). Your pile of 500 resumes should only take you about eight hours. OK, that's still a long time, but one day spent screening resumes to find the few jewels is time well spent. In my next book, I'll talk about how to develop the ability to stay awake during prolonged periods of boring reading …

Effective Interviewing

Spend a little honest time with yourself and think about the qualities you value and seek in your employees. What has worked for you in the past? What has caused problems? Everyone has their own list, but I have found that the following traits are common in the most successful QA people, regardless of their job titles: attitude, confidence, organization, maturity, empathy, curiosity, and a sense of humor.

It's fine to have a list of traits and qualities you're seeking. It really helps to have a list of interview questions that will help you ascertain if the candidate possesses those qualities. The following questions have worked well for me. Be sure to use questions that you are comfortable asking. Remember, it's fair for the candidate to ask you the same questions! Also, depending on your corporate environment, you may need to get your interview questions approved by your management or human resources department.

Attitude

Goal:
High energy, low maintenance

I want people with good attitudes! A mediocre person with a great attitude will go much farther than a very smart, qualified person with a bad attitude. Remember, your staff will have to work with this person. So will you. And killing your own employee is considered bad form, though it may be warranted. You need to ascertain if this person will be effective in your organization. Will they be high energy and low maintenance? Will this person fit in with your existing staff and with the staff you intend to have for the long run? Will the person take this job seriously? I've actually had people interview with me and tell me they wanted the QA position as a stepping-stone into development. Now that's someone who is not likely to take my job seriously and who will not understand the importance of good quality assurance in the production of a high quality, supportable product.

How do you determine if this person has the attitude you want? Here's a sample question:

- *What did you like/dislike about your previous job/manager?*

An honest answer to this question will tell you a lot about your candidate. Do their likes match the features your job and environment have to offer? Are their dislikes reasonable? Are those dislikes a part of your environment? I've heard people say they hated having to go to a developer's office with a bug. Hmmmm. Why? Did they not know enough to explain the problem? Were their developers unusually hostile? The likes and dislikes about their previous manager will also tell you a lot about how they will interact with you. If they liked their manager and had a good relationship with that person, you should expect to see that manager on the reference list. If they felt their manager spent too much time micromanaging, you probably want to find out your candidate's definition of micromanaging.

Confidence

Goal:
Confident but not arrogant

A good QA person has to be comfortable with their role and the job they are doing. If they don't have confidence, they will easily be deflected when they approach a developer with a problem. Like it or not, there is sometimes a certain amount of deference expected by senior developers. Is that deference acceptable? It depends. It is not unreasonable to be expected to defer to someone with superior knowledge and experience. I expect my team and the development team to treat each other with common courtesy and professionalism. Deference is one thing – being a doormat is another. Only a confident person can exhibit the right attitude while still getting their point across, and obtain the information they are seeking. Confidence does not mean arrogance. One of the fastest ways to fail in this industry is to be arrogant without the expertise to support it. There is always someone who knows more than you do. There are also those who like to think they know more than you do. For the most part that doesn't do any harm, as long as you have an effective working relationship.

Seeking Knowledge

QA is rarely afforded the same technology training opportunities as their development counterparts. As a result, QA people are often playing catch up when a new product arrives that employs a new technology. That means they sometimes have to ask what may be perceived as a "stupid" question. They must have the confidence to ask that question because they need the information.

As an aside, if you have training issues like this, you need to work to fix the problem. Are you getting an adequate training budget? If not, you need to fix the inequity. In order to perform good QA work, you must be trained in the technology. Without proper training, you lose credibility and good people. In some cases, you may need domain training, as well as technical training. This is particularly true if you have a staff of technical people who are removed from the end user. I have also been in the situation where we were given the same training opportunities as the development staff, but it was six months before we needed it.

Mice Need Not Apply

Now I'm looking at my candidate. I need someone to join my team who will be a strong member. I don't need a mouse. I don't need someone who will scurry into my office the first time a big, bad developer growls at them. I have no problem defending my people when they have been wronged, but I do expect them to form working relationships on their own.

There are some questions you should be able to answer at the conclusion of the interview. Will this person come across as competent and knowledgeable? Do they have the technical expertise to hold their own in a technical conversation? Will they know when to stand up for their work?

And, conversely, will they know when to admit they are wrong? Will I be able to send this person to a project meeting to represent QA? These are hard questions to answer and the answers are critical to your hiring decision.

The following interview questions will help you get the information you need to determine if the person has the characteristics mentioned above:

- *Give me examples of your normal interactions with former developers/ managers.*
- *Give me an example of a problem you have presented to your manager.*
- *How do you handle a developer who tells you, "It has to work that way because of the underlying technology which you obviously don't understand."?*

Honest answers to the above questions, or even answers made off the cuff, will tell you how this person interacts with their co-workers and managers. These are real world questions and you will tend to get an honest answer because the person will not have time to think up a politically correct answer. Each work environment is different, so you can expect the normal interactions to vary. Maybe the work situation requires that all interaction be done via email. Great. Ask if they've ever had a problem with a misunderstanding in email. Probably. See if they understand what caused the misunderstanding and how they fixed the situation. You're looking to see if this person can admit they have been wrong, which takes confidence. You will also find out how they dealt with a difficult developer, which everyone has encountered somewhere along the way. How creative were they? Did they run to their manager for help without trying to make inroads of their own? Good problem solving skills require confidence and creativity. I know I've got a good candidate when they smile at this last question – they've been there.

Organization

Goal:
Interruptions handled
efficiently in a multi-tasking
environment

Good QA work requires good organizational skills. Writing an accurate report requires a certain degree of meticulousness in keeping track of how the software behaves in various circumstances. A disorganized person will do disorganized testing, and while that may make them look busy, it won't contribute much to a managed environment where you can assess the work that has been completed. Almost everyone says they have good organizational skills, but you want to find out if this person has the specific organizational skills that are required for this job. Do they have a method to keep track of multiple tasks? Can this person be interrupted from a task and return to it later with minimal downtime?

Testing is a job with frequent interruptions. The work we do is set up that way. We write up a problem and move on. Just about the time we're deep into the next task, the developer needs more information on the problem report. We change gears, fulfill the information request, and switch back to the task at hand. This may happen several times until the final fix is obtained. And, if you do find a few spare minutes, there are always test cases to be updated, reports to be completed, and new bugs to be documented. The ability to be interrupted and pick up where you left off is a critical skill that we want to be sure our candidate is prepared for.

The first and most obvious interview question on this subject is to find out how many concurrent projects the candidate has successfully handled. If they've worked on multiple projects, you should get lots of input from them when you discuss the scenario above. In addition, ask them:

- *How do you remember the steps you took to find a bug?*
- *What methods do you use to keep track of meetings/appointments/interruptions?*

Each employee must develop methods that work for themselves. Personally, I'm a fan of the yellow-sticky notes system. I write lots of notes to myself on yellow stickies then place them on my desk in a position according by their urgency. This system works well for me. Sometimes, I even branch out to multiple colors! While it may not make for the most professional-looking desk, I don't forget things. Everyone should have some kind of system. Get the candidate to explain their system to you, and ask for examples of how it works for them.

Maturity

It is now time to do some honest analysis. What do you really expect from your candidate? Do you expect a junior QA person to approach a hostile developer with a questionable problem? What is your environment like? I once worked for an Internet startup company that was very much like working in a fraternity house. Add to that, I was the only female on the

Goal:
Effectiveness in the environment

technical staff. There weren't many rules in that company, and naked women on calendars were an accepted norm. I didn't have to stay there, but chose to do so because the technology was interesting. It did make me very conscious of whom I hired though.

This is nowhere near as difficult an environment as another Internet startup (to remain unnamed) where a new QA manager received a test of his maturity and his ability to handle a difficult situation. He arrived at his new job full of management zeal and excited to work with this team. He was soon approached by a woman employee who hemmed and hawed as she tried to explain the difficulties she was having with one of the developers. The following conversation ensued:

> MANAGER: "Is he unwilling to help you?"
> EMPLOYEE: "No."
> MANAGER: "Is he not listening to you?"
> EMPLOYEE: "No, that's not the problem at all."
> MANAGER: "Well, what is the problem then?"
> EMPLOYEE: "Well… he's in his office."
> MANAGER: "OK, is that a problem?"
> EMPLOYEE: "Not really."
> MANAGER: "Would it be better if he came to the lab to see the problem?"
> EMPLOYEE: (emphatically) "No, definitely not."
> MANAGER: "I don't understand the problem."
> EMPLOYEE: "Well, you see, uh, he's in his office and he's, uh, naked."

OK, now this is a difficult situation. The manager, utterly shocked, verified that the man was indeed working in his office unclothed, and he then went to the development manager. It turned out that this developer was considered critical to the company, was a personal friend of the CEO, and felt that he was at his creative best when unrestricted by clothing. The understanding when he was hired was that he could work in his office stark naked. After much discussion, and having come to the determination that there was no higher authority to which to appeal, we all agreed that the developer could continue to work in his office unclothed, but under no circumstances was anyone to request his presence in the lab!

Now that's the kind of situation to challenge anyone's maturity! Although you are unlikely to be hiring into a similar situation (I hope!), you still must consider the maturity of your candidate. Will you be comfortable with this person representing you and your department? Does this person have the leadership potential the position requires? Will this person be able to deal with interpersonal issues (e.g., naked people) in a professional manner? Try these interview questions to help you determine the answers to the previous questions:

- *What was the most difficult work situation you've encountered? How did you handle it?*
- *Have you ever had someone scream at you in a business situation? How did you handle it?*

With these questions, you are likely to learn a lot about the environments this candidate has worked in and how well they survived these experiences. You can extrapolate from that to see how they would do in your environment.

Empathy

Some of my very best QA people have previously worked in support and/or development. They have experienced the other side of the world. Good QA people need to be empathetic with the developer whose code they are testing, as well as with the customer who has to use it. You need to know if your candidate will be able to report a bug to a developer without causing offense. You also need to know if they will be able to see both sides of an argument about whether or not an observed behavior is actually a bug. If this person cannot step back and see the other person's point of view, you may end up having to deal with hurt feelings and overtly offensive behavior.

Goal:
Ability to see someone else's viewpoint

Empathy is a difficult characteristic to assess. Someone who is empathetic will be fair and will gain respect by their ability to be objective. This is very important in a good QA person and absolutely critical in anyone headed for management. Conversely, someone who is not empathetic may talk about the pleasure of "catching" or "embarrassing" developers. I like to ask the following questions:

- *How do you present a bug to a developer? Do you change your methods if there is a tight deadline?*
- *If you disagree with your manager, what do you do?*

I want to see that the candidate is interested in their manager's viewpoint. Even the most junior team member should be able to understand that they will disagree with their manager at one time or another, and they should be able to understand that their manager might have a point. Sometimes leading the conversation works here. If they offer an example from experience, ask why they think their manager acted as they did. Can they step back and look objectively at the issue?

Sometimes I'll slide down in my chair and say I'm tired. I want to see if they will sympathize with me. Empathy is a very hard characteristic to assess, but you sure want to have it in your candidate because it is very hard to train someone to be considerate of others.

Curiosity

Goal:
Driven by the need to know
"what happens if…"

Good QA people are curious. They want to know "what happens if …" Curiosity is what keeps the job interesting and it is one of the areas where we find our rewards. The worst QA people are those who don't wonder *why* something happens. They will become easily bored and will miss many problems by just accepting a program's behavior as correct without questioning it.

Unlike empathy, curiosity is fairly easy to assess, since you can tell by the questions they ask. This should be a two-way interview. Be sure you have created an environment in which questions are welcome, then sit back and think about the questions you are asked. When interviewing, I like to ask people what they like most about their job. Experienced QA people will often say they like to think up ways to break the software. Perfect! That's what I'm looking for: minds that are creative, realistic, and maybe a little bit devious.

To determine if the candidate has the right level of interest, I like to ask the following questions:

- *What is your favorite part of your job?*
- *What do you do when the software doesn't do what you expected?*
- *Do you enjoy troubleshooting?*
- *When you get a new software product, how do you figure out how it works?*

I want to see that the person doesn't just accept that the software works, but rather wants to prove that it does or doesn't. I want them to be interested in what they do and to look at each new project as a welcome challenge. Back to the concept of having the brains of the best developers; you have to enjoy the idea of outsmarting the designers and developers. It is part of the fun.

Sense of Humor

A good sense of humor can carry you through the tight schedules and depressing releases of semi-functional software (but that never happens, does it?). I want a team that can hang together, and sometimes that means having the ability to share a joke. During the interview, I will try to draw the person out to see if I can get them to smile or laugh. This does require getting them relaxed enough to loosen up during the interview. I want to know if this person can use appropriate humor to deflect a hostile developer. I once had a developer look at a bug report I'd written and say, "Well, no REAL person would ever do this!" From then on, anytime any member of my team went into his office, we prefaced the conversation with, "I know I'm not a real person, but…." He was amused that we thought it was funny, and it became a good joke within the team.

Goal:
Recognize and enjoy the humor that is inherent in the job

I also want to know if someone can see the humor in a situation. In a recent job, we had "schedule of the hour." While this really wasn't a joking matter, the unstable schedules had become so absurd there was nothing to do but treat them with amusement and continue on our planned path. This helped to disperse the anxiety that everyone was feeling over the volatile schedules. A positive attitude can get you through a lot of tough deadlines. Your best candidate needs to be able to carry through without becoming unproductively negative.

I only have one specific interview question for this area, but it's a very effective one:

■ *What's the funniest thing that's ever happened to you at work?*

The answer to this tells you whether the person's humor is appropriate and it can also make for good material for seminar presentations. Seriously though, funny things happen at work all the time. See if this person can recognize that fact and if they smile as they do so. You want someone who will enjoy their job and their co-workers. A happy work environment will produce a lot of good work.

Is Interviewing a Subjective Process?

You bet! Remember, in every interview session, you are interpreting the candidate's responses through your own experiences and prejudices. By now, you probably know how inaccurate that can make your assessment. So how can you combat this? You need to understand yourself, review your impressions, and see if you are being fair. Determine if your impressions, good or bad, are really relevant to the candidate's ability to perform the job.

But All Blue-Haired People Are Crazy!

It is reasonable to assume a person is on their best behavior during an interview

What do you do first? Recognize your own natural prejudices. Just because your crazy brother dyed his hair blue doesn't mean that all blue-haired people are crazy! Mannerisms and physical characteristics will often remind you of someone else – don't base your judgment on non-pertinent similarities. If a person reminds you of someone else, figure out why. I recently interviewed a person for a configuration management position. I immediately liked him and felt a positive connection with him. After he left the interview and I thought about it, I realized that my reason for the immediate positive impression was that he closely resembled an excellent system administrator who worked for me several years ago. Looking more closely at the impression he made on me, it was the physical resemblance that was striking, rather than his job skills. Probably not a good basis for a hiring decision! If he had reminded me of the other person because of the way he answered questions or his personality in general, those very well could have been positive characteristics to consider in the hiring decision.

You will tend to evaluate other people's actions within the framework of what it would mean if you did the same thing. Be conscious of this. I would never be late for an interview. I may be overly careful in that respect. If something happened that caused me to be late, I would probably rub my hands on my tire and claim I had a flat! Yet I have had candidates waltz in 30 minutes late for an interview without an explanation or an apology, even while confirming that they did have the right time for the interview. I really have a problem with someone who is late for an interview. Now, is this a fair indicator of their future job performance? I think it is. What if the same person showed up 30 minutes late to an executive staff briefing? Or a demo? That behavior would be unacceptable.

Fair or Unfair?

Let's look at some other examples of fair and unfair assumptions. What if a candidate refuses to make eye contact with you? Maybe he is very shy. If so, you need to work on drawing him out, and getting him to talk to you. Sometimes a long pause in the conversation will make the person look up at you. If you can't get him to consistently establish eye contact, you have to decide whether this is a potential problem. In some companies, body language is extremely important, and eye contact is considered a sign of honesty. The shy person is probably going to have trouble in those companies, depending on his position. If, on the other hand, the company likes people to stick to themselves, stay in their offices, and do their work, he might be a good fit. It's not enough that the person is a good fit for only the technical side of the job; he must also be a good fit within the organization.

What if your candidate is a 25-year-old, newly married woman? Uh-oh, she's in the baby years. Can you assume you know her family plans? Of course not. Early in my career I hired an administrative assistant who was eight weeks pregnant. There was no way I could have known. My boss came unglued, upset that I had made a stupid mistake in hiring her. He appeared to be right when she had to leave work a few months into the pregnancy. I waited anxiously to see if she would return to work or if my boss would be right and she would leave. I won. She did return to work and worked for me for the next eight years. Honestly though, if the situation had turned out the way my boss had predicted, I would have tended to be extremely cautious in any hires of candidates in "the baby years," though that would have been illegal. I would have had to overcome my prejudice in that area.

Everyone has been burned by a bad hire at some time in their career. Learn from your mistakes, but don't let those experiences unfairly color your judgment about future hires.

Interviewing – Getting Answers to the "Wrong" Questions

There are a lot of questions that you simply may not ask in an interview due to legal issues. Your HR department should have a list of those. In general, you can't ask any personal questions or any questions which are not related to the position in question. For example, you can ask if someone can travel or work overtime, but you can't ask what their childcare arrangements are. So, how do you find out the information that you really want to have but can't legally ask? It's easy – let the person talk! Create a relaxed and inviting environment. Tell them things about yourself. If I want to find out about someone's kids, I tell them about mine. They will usually reciprocate.

But, what do you do if you find out something that tells you this person is a bad fit for your team? You can't reject someone for "prejudicial" reasons. Well, you could, but you would be opening yourself and your company to a lawsuit. So what do you do? Turn the interview into a discussion of why the candidate isn't really well-suited for the job. It is best if the person leaves your office knowing that they will not get the job, and knowing why they are not qualified. I once had a candidate tell me that she'd been fired from a large aerospace company because of "severe behavioral problems." Yikes! Clearly this was not someone I wanted to hire. After this confession, I then spent the rest of the interview time explaining that I needed specific experience levels and that she just didn't meet my criteria. Even though she had volunteered this information, I didn't want her to later decide that I had turned her down strictly because of it. In truth, she did not meet my technical requirements for the job. I was lucky.

Behavioral Problems?

Don't forget to watch for subtle clues to behavioral problems. Excessive fidgeting could be an indication of a person who is extremely nervous, or it could be someone who just can't sit still. Would you like to work next to them in a lab all day? Have you ever interviewed someone who would not shut up? That person is not likely to be quiet on the job either. Some people will say inappropriate things about their former supervisor or co-workers in the interview, which shows a lack of common sense. For all they know, I might know those people. I like to give the candidate a tour of the facility. They should show an interest and ask some questions. These 45–60 minutes are all you will get to make your hiring decision, so use the time wisely and watch closely. Small observations may be indicative of future job performance.

Forming Opinions

Now it is time to decide what your opinion is of your candidate. Ask your-self; do you want to work with the candidate? If you don't, it's not fair to curse your team with this person. Some people would be good employees, but not good co-workers. What if you were demoted from your position tomorrow and this person would then be your equal? Could you work with them? It is always difficult to assess how someone will integrate with your existing team. If they won't mesh, you may be signing up for some signif-icant problems down the road. It's usually a good idea to have one of your team members interview your candidate. This does two things. You get an opinion from a future co-worker, and if the interviewer agrees to hire the candidate, you get a proponent already installed in your department.

Don't hire someone you don't want to work with

As soon as the interview is concluded, write down your notes and your thoughts about the candidate. Remember though, anything you write down can be subpoenaed later if the person decides there was unfair dis-crimination in the hiring process. Be sure you would be willing to defend, in court, anything you write.

Personally, I like to sleep on hiring decisions. The next morning, if I come in dying to hire somebody and afraid they'll get away, I proceed. If I'm feeling so-so, or against it, I don't proceed. For a so-so candidate, I store them away for future reference in case I have a job that's a better fit later on. I need that period of separation before I make my decision. If I liked the candidate and had a good rapport with them during the inter-view, I need the time away to objectively evaluate their job skills. You don't want to hire someone just because you liked them; you want to hire them because they are the best candidate for your job.

Interviewing for the Future

Keep a database of candidates you have interviewed. If you stay with the same or a similar job in the same area, you will see some people again and again over time. If their resume crosses your desk again, it helps to be able to go back and quickly check your notes. Also, be sure you keep the origi-nal resume and your notes on file where you can find them.

What if you can't hire the person right now, but you want them any-way? This happens in the rapidly changing world of software, where budg-ets may only stand for 24 hours. Be honest with your candidate – tell them why you can't hire them. Ask if you can call them at a later date for reconsideration. I once contacted someone a year and a half after the initial interview. She was still available and was happy to come back in for another interview for a new position that had just opened.

Make a Good Impression

Remember, people you don't want to hire may have friends that you do!

An interview should be a fact-finding experience for both parties. Your candidate should also be asking questions; maybe as many as you are asking. You want to be sure the interview process is a positive experience for both parties. Remember, even if you're not interested in this candidate, they might have friends that you would like to contact. When they walk out the door, they will tell their friends about their interview experience. Be sure they have good things to say.

Throughout the interview process, be honest about the position – good and bad. Also, be honest about the company. You want to see how this person reacts to the company's shortcomings. Do they see it as a challenge or do they run from the room screaming? Do they have realistic expectations? I have had people very honestly tell me that they wouldn't be comfortable working for my company when I told them we didn't actually know where all the source code was. On the other hand, the configuration management person that I did hire was thrilled with the prospect of hunting for the code and getting it all under control. To each his own! There's no point in luring someone into a job they won't like. They won't stay, and they'll resent you – and rightfully so.

Have you ever been on a bad interview? What made it bad? Would you ever go back to that company? What if you heard a friend was planning to interview there? Remember, when you are scheduling and conducting an interview, you are representing your company to that candidate and to everyone to whom they will talk. Be polite and professional. Treat your candidate with the consideration you would like to receive. Treat every candidate as a golden opportunity – some of them truly are. An interview should not be thought of as time spent, but as time invested.

Reference Checking

This is an area that's ripe with lawsuits. Most companies now prohibit their managers from giving references. In the past, the big concern was that you and your company could be sued if you gave a negative reference that caused an employee to be refused a job. Now there is the added concern that the hiring company may sue if they feel you gave a false-positive reference. It's a nasty world out there. In all honesty though, I feel obligated to give references for employees who have done a good job for me. As for people for whom I'd rather not give references, I tell them I can't. When giving references, be very careful. Be honest with what you are saying. Rather than saying something negative, tell the reference checker that you're not comfortable answering that question. They'll get the message.

What to Check For

So much for giving references. How about checking references? Let's face it, a positive reference doesn't really tell you much. I assume most of my candidates are smart enough to pick references that will stand behind them. Working on the assumption that the reference is going to try to put everything in a positive light, what can you ask that might give you some useful information? Instead of asking about weaknesses, ask about the person's strengths. A cagey reference will first ask what the position is so they can tailor the reference accordingly. In this case I will sometimes say that I'm considering the person for a couple of openings and I'm trying to evaluate their skills to see where they would fit best. If I do describe the job, I ask if this is something the candidate excels at, something they really enjoy doing. I ask if I can expect top performance in this job, or if the person would be better suited to another job. You can use this approach when checking manager and co-worker references. With managers, you should also try to establish a manager-to-manager relationship. How did this employee interact with you? What were their favorite tasks? What projects did you like to assign to them? You'll get a lot more information by starting a dialog in which you're asking for advice on how to manage this person.

Who to Check With

When collecting references, I find it's best to get a supervisor, a co-worker in the department, a co-worker out of the department, and a subordinate if you're hiring for a supervisory position. Ideally, you want to have references from several different jobs. Then you can look for patterns. People generally don't change a lot, but they may have been in different roles in different companies, so that can be useful information.

Providing you are allowed to do so, it is best to check the references yourself. HR departments tend to use a checklist and may not have the knowledge to tailor the questions for your particular position. For QA people, you want to be sure that they can get along with other groups. Listen for the subtle pauses when you ask questions like, "Did Bob ever have any issues dealing with developers?" Similarly, don't trust the reference list you get from a recruiter. Remember, they are pushing their candidate.

What about letters of reference? They're easily forged. Of course, you can check that, but do you have time? They are also open to interpretation. I recently read a letter of reference that included the following sentence: "I'd like to be able to recommend Betty for this job." Now what is that supposed to mean? He would like to recommend her, but professional ethics prohibit it? When you're checking references, you need to do it by phone. People are generally reluctant to send email and will be more willing to give additional information in a phone call. Establish a relationship with the person and get them to talk. Use the same techniques you used in conducting an interview.

After you've gathered all your reference information, be sure to write down what you've learned. Keep a copy of your reference notes with your interview notes; you may want to refer to them later to see whom you want to call back (and who to cuss out!).

Internal Referrals

Always conduct the same thorough interview process for an internal referral

Since we're on the subject of reference checks, what about internal referrals? In my career, I have been burned more times by internal referrals than any other kind of hire. What would motivate someone to refer a candidate who they know isn't qualified for the job? Who knows? It happens though, and you want to be sure you're not the unlucky one who hires the misfit. So, how do you guarantee that you don't fall into this trap? Conduct the same interview process as you would for an external candidate. Ask for external references and check them out. Just because someone sees fit to refer their fiancée for an open position, don't make the assumption that the person can do the job – interview thoroughly, and check their references as you would for anyone else.

4 Assembling the Parts to Construct Your Beast

So far we've discussed how to get yourself adapted to your new position, and how to hire people who will make you successful. Your team is probably composed of some employees you've hired and some employees you've inherited. Teams are always dynamic, so you can use the lessons learned about finding the best people throughout your career. Now that we know how to hire the right people, we need to develop them into a productive and effective team. In this section we'll talk about defining your team, including: defining your expectations for job classifications and individuals, matching the right person with the right position, and determining the correct number of members for your project teams. We'll also discuss how to identify and build good leaders. A department must have enough of the right kinds of people to get the work done. Even the tightest teams will have problems over time. Those problems may be due to people, projects, or even the company itself. As a manager, it is important that you recognize what makes your team work, how to build that team, and how to keep it together.

Defining Your Team

Generally in the computer technology industry, there are two terms used to define jobs: job classifications and job descriptions. Unfortunately, these terms are not used in a consistent manner. Therefore, for the sake of clarity, here's how I will use them. A job *classification* is the bit of information necessary to "classify" a job. It may consist of no more than a title and a number. Usually, it is used to define a salary range, perhaps an experience range, and little else. A job *description* actually explains the responsibilities and qualifications of the employee. There can be (and usually is) a significant overlap between these two. The following examples may help clarify this:

Figure 1:
Sample Job Classification

Job Classification:	Job Grade 38
Title:	Senior Software Engineer
Salary Range:	low $ 60,000–$ 80,000
	mid $ 80,001–$100,000
	high $100,001–$130,000
Years Experience:	Minimum five years
Degree: Technical	degree required

In the recruiting section of this book, I gave an example of a job description that could be used when soliciting resumes. Here we will look at an example that provides a more detailed job description. The level of detail to use will depend upon your situation. It's easier to complete performance evaluations when you have detailed job descriptions. It's harder to promote talented people who might not have <u>all</u> the stated job skills, yet are capable of doing the more advanced job. You have to decide what works best in your situation. Personally, I like the flexibility of the less-exacting job description like the one in the recruiting section. But if you prefer more detail, here is another example:

Job Description: Senior Software Engineer, Quality Assurance

Figure 2:
Sample Job Description

Job Summary: Understand and communicate the role of the Quality Assurance Team in detecting and preventing product defects. Implement Quality Assurance methodologies at the project and team level under the direction of the managing Quality Assurance Engineer.

Job Duties:
● Create summary and detail reports based upon test data, metrics, and trend analysis
● Design, configure, or create software test tools and perform application administration
● Act as a resource for the administration and maintenance of a QA test lab
● Create and publish test summaries describing product testing and issue resolution
● Conduct testing using the designated test methodologies
● Isolate software problems and produce clear and detailed defect reports
● Verify and close issues reported as fixed
● Create, execute, and maintain automated test scripts in assigned areas
● Create, execute, and maintain complex test cases for products and/or internal applications
● Suggest and implement innovative approaches for problem resolution
● Create, interpret, and supervise the reporting of test and error logs
● Create and maintain checklists and status reports
● Provide support and suggestions for continuously improving defect tracking and reporting
● Review and provide input on the accuracy and clarity of user documentation
● Create and supervise detailed reports for test data, metrics, and trend analysis
● Research and evaluate test tools

- Test products according to engineering and business specifications
- Work effectively in a multi-tasking and highly dynamic environment
- Organize and manage multiple (sometimes competing) tasks, priorities, and deadlines across departmental teams
- Provide significant input for QA documentation inspections
- Recommend product improvements
- Create, supervise, and maintain test plans, verifying consistency across products
- Develop significant expertise in the test environment, including operating systems, browsers, databases, network configurations, HTML, XML, Java, etc.
- Obtain expertise in design tools as needed to actively participate in design reviews
- Provide input to cross-departmental teams for document inspections, acceptance, and integration test cases
- Participate in software and database design meetings
- Suggest and implement improvements to processes and methodologies
- Continually improve knowledge of new technologies in the industry, including testing tools
- Train less-experienced staff members
- Perform other duties as assigned

Education Requirements:
- BS in Computer Science or other technical field

Experience Requirements:
- Four or more years experience as a Software Engineer in Quality Assurance

Additional Skill Areas:
- Working knowledge of software test methodologies
- Working knowledge of hardware and software systems, components, and multiple platform configurations
- Demonstrated analytical and investigative, problem-solving skills and the tenacity to work to the resolution of difficult tasks
- Demonstrated ability to assume responsibility for project assignments
- Excellent verbal and written communication skills
- Excellent time management skills
- Demonstrated ability to work independently

Figure 2:

Ideally, you want your job descriptions to work for recruiting, promotion evaluations, and performance evaluations. When you're considering how much detail to include, think about all the possible uses of the job description. If you're looking for examples of job descriptions, browse the web for some ideas. There are plenty out there.

Check the internet for examples of job descriptions.

Tailoring Job Descriptions

Your company may have HR-defined job descriptions, no descriptions at all, or just general classification categories. As you can see from the above example, a job classification is not going to be very helpful during a performance review. The job description, however, would be very useful.

Whatever your environment, you need to review the published job descriptions and determine if they accurately apply to the people you have in those positions. In addition to whatever is formally written for the job, you also need to write down your expectations for each job. If that means you are writing your own job descriptions for each of the generally defined job classifications, so be it. It's better to have something in writing than to be evaluating people against criteria that may be subjective and variable.

The other advantage of tailoring your own job descriptions is to allow you to accurately describe your expectations for people in those positions. By writing this down and making it available to your staff, you have established their expectations for the things you will be evaluating when it is time for their performance review. You've also set the bar for people seeking promotions. And remember, job descriptions may change over time as the department, processes, and policies change. For example, you may be in the early stages of implementing QA involvement in requirements reviews. Because it's a politically sticky situation, you only want your senior product experts in those meetings. As a QA presence becomes more expected and accepted, you can make requirements reviews a part of every Senior Engineer's job. It is important to keep job descriptions up-to-date.

If you are the one writing the job descriptions for the first time, you might want to look at some examples. Look at the ones your company has been using. See what the development group is using. One bit of caution though; when you indicate required years of experience, be careful about specifying ranges. Don't say that an Engineer should have 3–5 years of experience and a Senior Engineer should have 5–7 years of experience. If that is the only criteria, everyone will expect a promotion at their fifth year, and may wonder what happened if you promote someone early. Remember to take into account all the job factors, such as maturity, responsibility, technical skills, and the positive application of those skills.

Tailoring for the Individual

In addition to clearly defining and communicating your expectations for each job, you also need to define and communicate your expectations for each person working in your department. I emphasize "communicate" because it doesn't do any good to keep a beautiful set of pristine job descriptions that you only show at review time. (I discuss methods for conducting effective performance reviews in a later chapter.) These job descriptions are not meant to be solely assessment tools, but should be used for guidance and career development as well. To serve that purpose, you have to share the information with those affected by it. Each individual fits somewhere in a job classification, but you also have specific expectations for that person. You see their strengths and weaknesses as well as their potential.

Let's look at how our job descriptions could help us plot someone's career path. Let's say I have a Senior Engineer named Joe, who has excellent technical skills but is weak in the project management area. Now I have to look at where I want Joe to go, and where he wants to go as his career develops. As I look at my career chart, I can see that Joe has two paths available for him: Management or Technical.

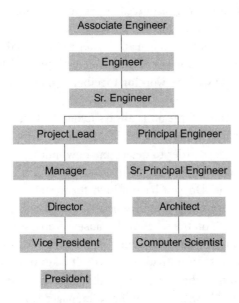

Figure 3:
Sample Career Chart

I look at my trusty job descriptions and find that one of the primary responsibilities for a Project Lead is to handle personnel responsibilities. Uh-oh. Joe doesn't actually like people; therefore, this could be a problematic path for him. On the other hand, he is very strong technically and could be successful on the technical path. How does he see himself? We need to discuss this when we talk about his career goals. I can use my job descriptions to help Joe see the responsibilities that each position will entail. This will help him make an intelligent career choice and will help me know what training I should be arranging so Joe can succeed in advancement. Certainly, he and I need to agree on where his career is going so we can work together to get him there. The only way this can happen is with open communication. The job description discussion is a great way to start down this road.

Putting the Right People in the Right Positions

We don't require people with perfect skills – but our team needs to have a perfect skill mix

You may not have the staff you need to build your ideal team. I think I might have had that perfect team once, a very long time ago. Or maybe I just dreamed it. Since it is unlikely to happen, assume you're not going to have everyone you need. Begin by fitting the people you do have into your ideal model, and then figure out what's missing. If the holes are critical, you need to procure some resources or get busy training. A highly motivated team can get extra work done, so maybe you can squeeze an extra man-week of effort out of your team if they're interested in what they're doing. Remember, you don't need 10 people with perfect skills – you need a team of 10 people who, by working together, can deliver the perfect skill mix.

The composition of a team is always dynamic. Overlapping skills are required, but you may have to trade off the security of overlap for a broader skill range. In order to determine how much risk you can take in having people with unique and critical skills, look at how stable your team is likely to be. Do you have a high turnover? Will people have to move onto other projects? If movement is likely, you need to plan for cross training. Put it on the schedule because it won't just happen by itself. People need to know that the training is important for the company, for the project, and for their individual growth. It takes time, and if you don't make the time in the schedule, people will tend to stay with the areas they are most comfortable with. Your job as a manager is to root them out of their safe dens and get them trained, for your sake as well as theirs. We'll explore the specifics of training and creating a good training program in Chapter 11.

Mapping People to Projects

So let's say we have our team and our project list. How about a simple way to map one to the other? I'm a great believer in keeping simple project plans. I've been involved in organizations that devoted entire jobs to tracking projects. For my own scheduling and resource management though, I prefer a very straightforward spreadsheet. The first thing I do is break my project into the major tasks or phases. Then, I look at the skill sets required to get the work done on those tasks. Next, I map my needs against what I have. By this time I usually have to go to lunch to recover. Seriously though, by mapping each project in this manner, I can combine my projects and my resources into a scalable management tool. I used this method when I was managing a QA department with 45 people and 14 concurrent projects, and I'm still relatively sane.

The following is an example that shows a rough resource schedule for two new projects, one maintenance project, support for a tradeshow, on-going customer support, and an outsourced localization project. For the sake of simplification, we won't consider the non-testing utility people such as system administrators, configuration managers, etc., but those folks are usually divided up as percentages across all the projects.

First, we have to figure out the components of the projects. Then, we have to figure out how many people will be needed to get the necessary work accomplished for each component. I generally look at three-month schedules; anything beyond that is usually fiction. Obviously, for a long-term project, it is best to have a schedule on paper, or your management will wonder what you do all day. In truth though, if you are managing multiple projects, resources will shift around significantly as time goes on. Go ahead and map out the longer-term projects using this same method, but expect to do some later editing and concentrate your refining efforts to the three-month time frame.

Scheduling beyond three months in the future usually falls in the realm of fiction writing

The above chart is very simple and the categories are fairly general, but this is a useful planning tool. You can add as much detail as you need so that you feel you are getting an accurate picture of your project. One of the beauties of keeping your planning documents high-level is that you have to do a lot less maintenance. Maintaining your planning documents should not take longer than doing the actual planning.

Figure 4:
Sample Project Map

	January				February				March			
	Week 1	Week 2	Week 3	Week 4	Week 1	Week 2	Week 3	Week 4	Week 1	Week 2	Week 3	Week 4
New Project 1												
Design	1	1										
Automation Design		1	1									
Test Planning		1	1	1								
Auto Implementation				2	2	2						
Functional Testing					3	3						
Integration Testing							3	3				
System Testing									4	4		
Project Wrapup											2	
New Project 2												
Test Planning					1	1						
Functional Testing						2	2					
Integration Testing								2	2			
System Testing										2	2	
Project Wrapup												1
Maint Project 1												
Project Planning			1									
Functional Testing				1	1							
Regression Testing						1						
System Testing							2					
Project Wrapup								1				
Trade Show												
Product Test		1										
Product Doc Review		1										
Show Support			1									
Field Support	1	1	1	1	1	1	1	1	1	1	1	1
Localization												
Outsource Selection						1	1					
Outsource Planning								1	1			
Supervision										1	1	1
Documentation Review												1
TOTALS	2	6	5	5	8	11	9	8	8	8	6	4

Now that you know what tasks need to be accomplished, you can figure out what kinds of people can do those tasks. Again, keep it high-level. For a start, you can simply assign job titles to each task; this makes it easier later if you need to move people around between projects while keeping the same skill mix. Once we know the type of people we need for each task, we can use our handy spreadsheet format to determine the total numbers.

	January				February				March			
	Week 1	Week 2	Week 3	Week 4	Week 1	Week 2	Week 3	Week 4	Week 1	Week 2	Week 3	Week 4
New Project 1	1	3	2	3	5	5	3	3	4	4	2	
New Project 2					1	3	2	2	2	2	2	1
Maint Project 1			1	1	1	1	2	1				
TradeShow		2	1									
Field Support	1	1	1	1	1	1	1	1	1	1	1	1
Localization						1	1	1	1	1	1	2
TOTALS	2	6	5	5	8	11	9	8	8	8	6	4
Test Technician	0	0	0	0	1	2	3	2	2	2	1	0
Test Engineer 1	1	1	1	2	3	4	3	2	2	2	1	1
Test Engineer 2	1	1	1	1	2	2	2	3	2	2	2	1
Test Engineer 3	0	3	2	1	1	1	0	0	1	1	0	0
Test Lead	0	1	1	1	1	2	1	1	1	1	2	2
Total Needed	2	6	5	5	8	11	9	8	8	8	6	4
Test Technicians	0	0	0	0	2	2	2	2	2	2	2	2
Test Engineer 1	2	2	2	2	2	2	2	2	2	2	2	2
Test Engineer 2	2	2	2	2	2	2	2	2	2	2	2	2
Test Engineer 3	1	1	1	1	1	1	1	1	1	1	1	1
Test Lead	2	2	2	2	2	2	2	2	2	2	2	2
Total Have	7	7	7	7	9	9	9	9	9	9	9	9

Figure 5:
Skills Required Chart

In the above chart, we're assigning the following responsibilities by job classification:

Job Classification	Responsibilities
Test Technician	Test
Test Engineer 1 (Junior)	Automation, Test, Field Support
Test Engineer 2 (Senior)	Design, Test, Maintain Plan, Outsource Docs
Test Engineer 3 (Principal)	Automation, Test, Trade Show
Test Lead	Test Planning, Outsource

Figure 6:
Responsibility Chart

Now we can compare what we need against what we have. For example, in the second week of February, we need eleven people but have only nine. There are some options to consider: Can we move one of the projects to eliminate the overlap, or can we use more senior people to get the work done and perhaps do it more quickly than a junior person? Could Project 2 start a week later and remove the high load in that week? Or could the localization start a week later?

While these plans won't completely eliminate the bottleneck, they will help some. Through playing around with the schedule and applying a different skill mix, you can usually accommodate most projects, assuming your department is generally the right size. (We'll talk more about that later in this section.) This chart is also helpful in determining the skills that you will need in the future. If I find that I'm short on Test Engineer 3's which will be needed for the upcoming automation projects, I know I need to get busy with training. I can also use this chart to map my specific skill sets to specific projects. For example, does Project 1 need Unix system administration skills? Do I have someone to do that?

Picking Your Leads

If you have multiple projects, or subprojects within a project, keep in mind that you'll need people to lead. In my terminology, a "lead" is a person who has project and personnel responsibility. In some organizations, leads never have personnel management roles, only project responsibility. In reality, the amount of project and personnel responsibility varies with the person and the project. Leads are people just like the people they are leading; they have strengths, weaknesses, and areas of comfort. To determine who should lead a project, consider the size of the project, the experience level of those being managed, the experience level of the proposed lead, and the expected technical involvement of the lead. All of these factors must be considered before selecting your lead.

A very experienced group will need less guidance. In fact, they may resent too much guidance. While it is tempting to use an inexperienced lead with a more experienced group, you may be bringing on unwanted personnel issues. Senior people expect more autonomy and will be unhappy if your inexperienced lead tries to impose too much control. However, an inexperienced lead with great people skills can effectively manage a project with senior people. Conversely, a strong technical lead with less developed people skills can effectively manage a group of junior people. They will need the technical guidance and respect the lead for giving it, while also being more tolerant of less-developed people skills.

Good leaders have several characteristics:

■ The ability to train others
■ Interest in career development of their staff
■ The desire and ability to lead
■ Technical capabilities as required by the organization

You can't teach someone to have these non-technical attributes. You can hone the abilities they have, but you're not going to teach someone to care about their people or to be a genuinely good trainer. If your chosen candidate does not have the first three skills on the list, rough though it may be, you should start looking for someone else.

This brings up the next issue. Can you afford to make a lead out of a strong technical contributor? If you can't, then you haven't planned carefully enough. It is unfair to deny someone a promotion because you don't have anyone to backfill for them. Sometimes you need to make that part of the deal: "I'll promote you in six months provided you train Tom to take over your technical duties."

But if I promote you, who will do all the work?

It's not fair to add management responsibilities on top of someone's technical duties without offloading some of their work. To overload someone in a new position is setting them up to fail. Also, when people are overwhelmed, they tend to retreat to working on the areas in which they are most comfortable. It's difficult for a strong technical person to make the transition to management. As we've discussed, the reward system is different and the perception of the individual contribution is gone. As a result, if a strong technical person is faced with an impossible workload, they'll return to doing their technical tasks and avoid the new management responsibilities. The result will be an ineffectual lead who will fail, and no one will be happy. You have to plan for the career growth of each person, particularly those you are grooming for management.

Will Your Lead Stack Up?

When you are selecting your lead candidates, be sure they are as technically competent as their development counterparts. Now, "technically competent" does not necessarily mean they're going to be wrestling Java code into submission. It does mean that they need to be able to understand the product architecture and the technical aspects of the projects that affect testing. How technical? It depends on the environment. I've been in some places where the QA leads were expected to attend and actively participate in code reviews. I've been in others where the participation was limited to very high-level product discussions. I've also worked in environments where a particular tool was used, and QA was expected to speak and understand that tool's terminology. So, in reality, the need for technical competence is highly variable. You have to determine the demands of your environment and then get the appropriate people trained to the level required.

No Training Budget

What? No training budget (still?)? Here's a golden opportunity to get close to the development group. Ask them what your leads should know in order to be effective. This does two things for you:

1) Development has to think in terms of how QA could actually be useful in design reviews, which may be a completely new thought for them.
2) After they tell you what your folks need to know, you can ask them how to get that training. If classes aren't feasible because of timing or budget, ask if development will help with on-the-job training (OJT). They almost have to say yes. Once they're part of the training effort, they'll be more patient and instructive as the project evolves.

It is important for leads to have technical competency to gain the respect they deserve, and to provide them with the skills they need to effectively accomplish their job. Be sure your managers are as technically competent as their development and project management counterparts. In later sections, we'll talk about developing skills within your group and creating a career-conscious training system.

Technical vs. Managerial Training

Is there a point in your career when technical knowledge is no longer important? Once again, this depends on your environment and your comfort level. I once had a job as a QA Director where my technical knowledge and skills truly didn't matter. In that position, my administrative skills – public speaking, organization, strategic planning – were what I used. Exclusively. It was a really boring job to me. It was also the only job I ever had where my technical knowledge was not used. So how do you know what you need to know? Look around you. How technical are your peers? You need to be able to match up. Also look at how technical your boss is. Technical people value technical skills.

I once worked for a VP who was a strong programmer. When he started with the company, he locked himself in his office and read all the source code. Wow. When he emerged, somewhat bleary-eyed, he met with each of the 30-odd developers and discussed their code with them. They were impressed and a little unnerved. This was obviously not someone they were going to con. For all the time I worked with him he had the complete respect and devotion of his group. Wouldn't we all like that? So how do you stay current technically? Read. Take some classes. And, most importantly, ask questions and learn on the job. Technology changes very quickly and it takes significant effort to keep up. On the bright side, some of those books will cure your insomnia!

What about management training? It should be obvious by now that I've learned a lot from my mistakes. But, that is a painful and sometimes career-limiting path to progress. There are certainly some good management training courses and books (like this one, right?). Just remember to use the reality filter on what you learn. There are few things more annoying than a manager who changes his management style as often as the pages of his day planner. Stick with a management style that makes you comfortable. Don't try to emulate someone else unless his or her style fits your personality. By all means though, watch and learn from others – both good and bad. Sometimes you learn more from a bad manager than a good one. It can be difficult to determine what makes a good manager successful, but as with gleaning technical information, observe, ask questions, and always leave room to learn.

You can learn a lot from a bad manager about what you should not do!

5   Fitting Your Beast into the Herd

It's one thing to have a finely built, cohesive team with the right skills and the right leadership. But how do we fit our perfect beast into the herd that is the entire organization? In this section we'll discuss several different organizational structures and the pros and cons of each. We'll also look at how to make these structures work effectively. In addition, we'll look at how to size the QA department itself and investigate some of the factors that can determine what the "right" size is.

Organizational Structures

There are two common organizational structures in the industry today. In the first, QA reports up through the development hierarchy as shown below:

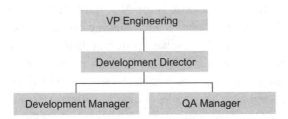

Figure 7:
Development-centric Organization

The Good:

It is easier to stay in the project loop because schedules and project problems are usually discussed freely. Since everyone is in the same boat, project problems tend to generate "team" resolutions.

The Neutral:

This is a very schedule-driven environment, which can be good or bad. It's good if there is recognition that quality assurance implemented early in the project will result in a more accurate, achievable, and accelerated schedule.

It's bad if the QA recognition is not there, and testing is seen as an imped-
iment to releasing the product.

The Bad:

The above-mentioned schedule-consciousness can be very bad. A development organization is usually focused on how many features they can
cram into a release before the deadline. Developers tend to be optimistic
about how much time will be required to implement these new, cool, and
imminently desirable features. The result? The development manager is
faced with having to stop implementing features (some of which may
already have been promised to customers) in order to allow adequate time
for the planned testing. Or, he could lean on you (the test manager), to
accept some late features and abbreviate your testing. And who is it that
does your performance review and approves your pay raises? Hmmmm.
How self-sacrificing are you willing to be?

Reward Systems

It's rare to find an organization structure like this which doesn't get caught
in such problems. The reward system for most development groups is
based on implementing features and shipping on time. QA is rewarded
based on the quality of the resultant products. Unfortunately, these goals
often conflict. And, as we've discussed, you'll be more successful if you
align your goals with your boss's goals. So what should you do? Educate!
Chances are, your boss knows a lot about development (we hope!) and not
as much about QA. It's time to teach him. Time to get out the cost of quality
analysis (see Figure 14: Cost Area Affected Based on Phase of Discovery/
Resolution) to show how much money and time can be saved by finding
bugs earlier.[1]

Using our Cost of Quality and Risk Analysis, now is the time to show
him you understand the importance of meeting the schedules while producing a quality project. Get out your metrics showing how products have
performed in the field, along with your analysis of what could be done to

---

1. For a good discussion of cost of quality and a useful example, refer to *Managing the
Testing Process* (Wiley, 2002) by Rex Black. Cem Kaner's book *Testing Computer Software* (Wiley, 1999) also has a good example showing the rising cost of fixing bugs in
later stages in the lifecycle.

alleviate the problems that are being seen. Here's where you show your quality risk analysis and your test case mapping. This shows what you've tested, and perhaps more importantly, what you didn't.

Now you can talk objectively about where the test time goes. Work with your manager to discuss where testing can be reduced (by implementing unit testing, code reviews, etc.) or increased, and the schedule implications of each case. It is sad but true: people want to assume that the software works. If development has done a good job, the software will work. If the software doesn't work, the test team did a bad job. And remember, "doesn't work" can mean the customer's requirements aren't met, usability issues make the software too hard to use, or even something as peripheral as the help text being incomplete.

Does your development-oriented boss understand all this? Probably not. Before you accept abbreviated schedules and excessive overtime as facts of life, you need to come to a real understanding with your boss about what the job is and what it isn't. You have a tremendous advantage in this organizational structure because the development manager is responsible for you, and that includes being responsible for quality. He can point his finger at you, but in the end that finger is back in his own face.

Other Areas That Affect Us

As long as we're talking about organizational structure here, let's explore some of the peripheral but critical functions that affect the quality of a release.

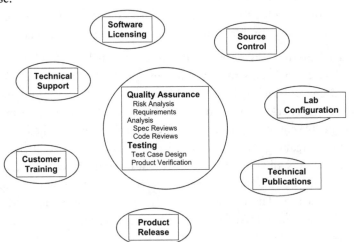

Figure 8:
Functions That Affect Release Quality

In my career, I have seen failures in each of the above satellite functions that caused a product release to fail due to "quality problems." Following are some examples taken from my personal experiences:

Software Licensing – No one took responsibility for the software licensing of a product I worked on. It became apparent after we shipped a release with another company's licensed software within it. When we finished paying the license fees, we ended up paying more money than we were making on the product. We tried to pass this cost on to our customers who promptly returned the software to us.

Source Control – Without good source control, you never really know what you are testing. You can lose valuable days, or even weeks of testing by using the wrong release – or the wrong compiled version.

Lab Configuration Management – I had a product fail abysmally in the field when it was installed on a version of an operating system we had never used in testing. Oops!

Documentation – Do you ever use the help text for a product? Do you ever read the manual? You expect it to be correct, don't you? I once had the documentation department ship the manuals straight to the customer prior to QA review (they were late, of course). There was only one significant error in the manuals. Unfortunately, the error was in the example installation script where it instructed the user to answer "yes" when it should have been "no." Did the software work correctly? Yes. Did the customer think it worked correctly after they had to endure a painful recovery, and three days of down time on a production system to uninstall and re-install? Not in the least. And whom did the VP of Sales want to talk with about this "quality" problem? It wasn't the documentation manager …

Product Release and Control – One time, we tested the "final" version of the software which contained fixes for three "must fix" problems. We were good to go. Unfortunately, the developer who made the midnight fixes neglected to check in his code. More unfortunately, when the product release people cut the release disks, one of the sales people picked up a copy (obviously breaking a rule) and hand-delivered it to a critical client that immediately installed it – all before we ran the final check on the release disks. About the time we discovered the error, the customer was on the phone to the president of our company, more than a little incensed about the major bugs our release had introduced into his production system. Our fault? No. Our blame? You bet.

Customer Training – If you have a complicated product or system, you may have mandatory customer training. This is a great idea as long as the training group is teaching about the latest features. That means someone has to tell them about the latest features...

Customer Support – Have you ever had a customer support job? I have. It can be thankless, frustrating work. It's also a very necessary job. I once got a call from a support engineer asking me if we'd just shipped a new release and if it had any new features. "Why yes," I proudly said. "It has a number of great new features." There was silence on the other end of the phone. Then, "When was someone going to tell us?" This wasn't my job, but I can imagine how foolish they felt and how incompetent they sounded when the customers had questions about features the support team had never seen. As a company, we had certainly made a negative impression on that customer (who paid a lot of money in maintenance fees expecting to get someone knowledgeable on the phone).

These functions are generally not considered to be within the realm of testing or QA. Even if you don't control these areas, it is critical that you coordinate closely with them. Quality is a company-wide concern, and as part of your efforts to educate, don't forget to include all the peripheral functions. If they fail, so do you.

Now that I completely diverged, let's return to the other common organizational structure. In this one, QA does not report through the development chain, but through another entity equal to the top of the development group. Here is an example of this:

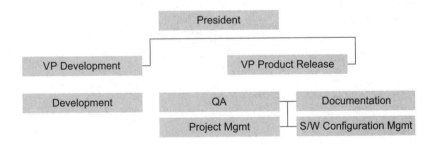

Figure 9:
Product-centric Organization

The Good

A product-centric organizational structure is good because release of the total product is the goal of this organization. Your pursuit of quality aligns well with your boss's goals. He has a view independent of the feature/

schedule push of development. In this situation, the needs of QA are not subordinate to the needs of development – you are truly equal organizationally and your boss has the same power as the development boss. This organizational structure is excellent for ensuring that quality receives its fair share of attention in high-level discussions. Of course, the success of this organization (as with the other), is still highly dependent upon the individuals within it. But it tends to favor quality more than the development-centric organization. There is also an advantage to having project management (PM). PM (if effective) has the overall project view, and is often the keeper of the schedule and budget. It is helpful to have them close to home, where they can gain a good understanding of your needs and efforts.

The Bad

A product-centric organizational structure is bad because quality is separate from development, and there can be a tendency for the "us vs. them" mentality to take root. It can be more difficult to insert QA functions into the development cycle because of this separation.

Project-centric Organization –
Administrative Report to Central QA Group

Figure 10:
Project-centric Organization
with Central QA Group

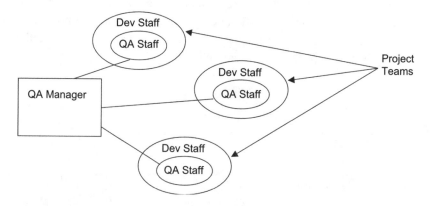

Project-centric Organization – No Central QA Group

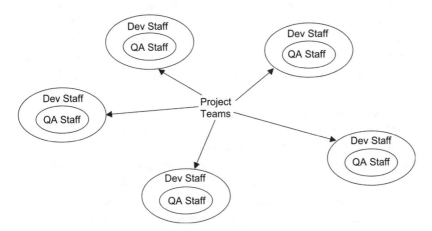

Figure 11:
*Project-centric Organization
with No Central QA Group*

Should QA Be Distributed?

At some time in your career, you may be faced with people who want to divide up the QA department and assign the project teams to development managers or project managers. Yikes! There are certainly some compelling reasons not to do this. And, while these reasons may be obvious to us, it might be worthwhile to point them out to your management. This structure is similar to putting the entire QA department under a development manager; only worse. The divide-and-conquer mentality that tends to fuel this organizational structure is sometimes effective in defeating the very purpose of the QA organization – to produce a quality product. "Agile Methods" and "Extreme Programming" are currently encouraging this type of structure. Before you hop on the bandwagon with the rest of the management, be sure to understand what you're doing to your people.

Think about it. If you're a QA guy, and you now report directly to a development manager, what are your goals? To ensure a quality product, or to stay on schedule? Let's face it. QA is a different function than development with different people and different goals. To merge the two functions into a single reporting unit is like asking the monkey to watch the bananas. The future is dim for the bananas. The software may be released on time, but will it meet the corporate quality standards?

In my opinion, a monolithic QA department is more effective, assuming it's managed correctly. By having one pool of resources, you can offer a service to the various development groups and projects. You can share

A well-managed monolithic QA department is more effective

resources efficiently between projects and move skill sets as needed without worrying about crossing administrative boundaries. QA, like configuration management, needs to supply a consistent product to all the groups it services. In this case, the product is quality assurance and testing. QA can be the unifying structure with an IT group that has multiple development units. Standards and processes can be created and enforced via the QA group.[2]

Organizational structures vary widely from company to company, and sometimes within a single company. Some folks swear by the project-based organization (which can exist within either of the above structures), where test teams are assigned to development groups on a project basis. Administrative reporting for the testers may also change from project to project. In this case of matrix management, it is extremely difficult for people to feel that there is any hope of career planning as they are shuffled from leader to leader, each intent only on meeting his short-term project deadlines. It is also difficult to coordinate sharing resources and planning for the future with this scenario because the teams tend to become islands. In the case where administrative reporting goes back to a central QA manager, the individual has the consistency and security of a single, long-term manager; the variety of changing projects; but the variability of frequently changing project managers who are making daily assignments. If the project mangers are good and the administrative manager stays in touch with the individuals, this can be an ideal situation providing flexibility, security, and keeping teams focused on their goals. If the project managers are bad, this, like any organization with bad management will fail and frustrate everyone involved.

There are many organization types. Environments may change over time with different staff and different projects. Any of them can work for the right people with quality-oriented goals. Also, any of them can fail with the wrong people or the wrong goals. Personally, I prefer the product-centric structure with a single QA organization that works on multiple projects. I think this provides maximum flexibility for cross-training, covering resource shortages, and keeping a global quality focus. That does not

---

2. But you'll want to be careful with this approach. Some people may see a monolithic testing group as a malignant bureaucracy to be avoided at all costs. Robert Sabourin wrote an article called "At Your Service" which is on www.stickyminds.com. In it, he discusses building a service organization that creates information products and services that are desired by the internal customers. Getting people to desire your products and services would be far better than having to force your products upon them.

mean the other types of organizations can't be equally as usable and flexible. It's a matter of where you can be most comfortable and effective, and where your people can be most comfortable and effective.

Determining The Right Size For Your Organization

So much for discussing the world we live in but probably don't control. Back to thinking about our own beast. We've talked about skill mixes and training needs. But how many people do we need? Figuring out the right size for your organization is never an easy task. Often, you are not given the option of dictating the number of people you have. Sometimes you don't even get input into the type of people you have. Still, someday, someone just might ask you. More likely, someday you'll be trying to justify adding a person to the department.

In this section I will discuss ways to determine the number of people you need along with some additional factors to be considered. The effectiveness of project management, the long-term relationships between the developers and your staff, outsourcing, and sales/support involvement are all factors that affect your workload. We'll also look at proportion allocation as a sizing method. Each environment is unique and circumstances vary over time. Take the following information as input to your decision-making process, but tailor it to your specific situation.

Project Management Considerations

In this context, I'm referring to Project Management as a third party (independent from development and QA) who has oversight responsibilities for your project(s). Good project management throughout a project will result in better-managed resources, a predictable schedule, and a smooth information flow. A well-managed project makes the QA job much easier. Schedule slippages are known and published, and the outcome discussed before the firefight begins. Budget pressures are managed by a separate entity who is concerned that BOTH development and QA have the resources they need to get the project done. If this project management entity is competent and strong, QA in general – and you in particular – can concentrate on the QA work that needs to be done. The schedule and budget responsibilities are only of concern within the QA world, not the overall project schedule and budget. Don't get lazy though, it always pays

If PM is competent and strong, we can concentrate on our own work

to know what's going on with master schedules and budgets even if you are not responsible.

Another significant advantage to strong project management is the channel for delegation. Stuff happens. Equipment may not get there on time. The software may be delivered on time but doesn't work. You may need to hire three contractors instead of two. If you have a strong project manager, you can delegate these kinds of issues to them and let them worry about the details and the approvals. You should just make your case; a valid one of course, and let them figure out how to get you what you need. Then go back to doing your daily work. Another beauty of strong project management is they become the primary reporting path to upper management. That means fewer meetings for you! You still have to gather and supply the useful information to be presented at these meetings, but you don't have to physically sit through the potentially mind (and posterior) numbing presentations on other projects that don't interest you.

On the other hand, if you have weak project management, you're going to have to do more work. When do schedule slips and budget overruns become most obvious? Toward the end of the project. Schedule slips show up when a major deliverable is missed (like the ship date). Budget overruns are apparent when the money is all spent and you ask for more. Unfortunately, since testing tends to be at the end of the food chain, that's where the software is when the bad things happen. If you don't have project management looking out for the project's overall interests (including QA), then you will have to be the defender against encroachment on your schedule and budget. That means sticking your nose into the project status well before testing begins.

I worked for a company that decided to hire ten contractors to assist their ten developers in developing a product. After the development was finished, the ten contractors were to move to QA to assist the four existing QA people. Except for the problem of having to assimilate and train ten contractors to do QA, this was deemed an acceptable solution to the schedule problems. As you can imagine, it didn't work out quite as planned. The schedule continued to slip due to design issues, and the ten contractors stayed in development two months into when they were supposed to move to QA. When the time finally came for them to move, development was declared complete. The money ran out, and the contractors were terminated. This left the four-person QA department wrestling with the unstable code developed by twenty developers, ten of whom were gone. The product finally shipped to beta four months later than the original GA (General Availability) date.

The lesson here? There is only one project budget and only one schedule. We may have our own schedule and budget within the master project schedule and budget, but in the end, there is only one that matters.

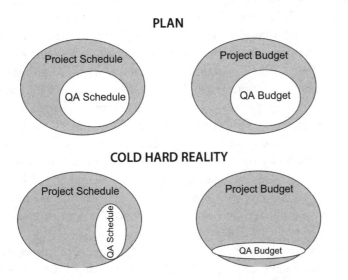

PLAN

Figure 12:
Realities of Schedule and Budget

COLD HARD REALITY

If you don't have someone watching out for your interests, you need to watch out for yourself. Don't let development burn up the schedule and money without raising the distress flags. The project will have problems, and you will be the one in charge when they become apparent. You need to stay alert enough to identify and notify when the problems first occur. Not only will this make you part of the project team and part of the solution, it will also alert them early enough so that remedies can be made before the problem becomes entirely yours.

One other word of caution: When things go wrong on a project, someone is expected to be accountable. If the schedule is perceived to be slipping on your watch, you can count on spending a significant amount of time in meetings explaining what happened. Time spent in meetings means time spent away from your "real" work. If this is an inevitable situation in your company, budget the time for it. And be sure you have done your quality risk analysis and have excellent test case tracking tools, so you can give management an accurate assessment of where you are versus where the schedule indicates testing should be.

Assigning People to Projects

Leverage the existing working relationships

I have had excellent success with informally teaming QA people with developers. This simply means I try to assign my people to work with the same sets of developers over time and projects. Sometimes this is done formally by declaring my QA person as the lead or the Primary Person Responsible (PPR) for a subsystem of the project. Sometimes it's as informal as "you test what Mark and Tom release." This works well if you have a central QA department that serves all projects. By matching QA folks with developers, you can maintain the good working relationships that have to be built over time. If people have worked together before and they enjoy working together, they can more easily move to new projects. Training will happen in a comfortable environment because the relationship is secure. The get-acquainted period is no longer necessary. This method provides excellent growth opportunities because the project team moves together onto new technologies and projects, keeping the work interesting and the personnel problems minimal. As a manager, this method allows you to make progressively more accurate schedules because you can predict how the project will unfold.

Match QA skill sets to developer skill sets

If you don't have the consistency in staffing to use the above strategy, you need to assign your people carefully. I like to match my most technical people with the most technical developers. This accomplishes two things. The most technical people are likely working on the most difficult code, so you'll need your best people concentrating on those areas. Also, by keeping skill sets matched, your people can talk to the developers as equals. If there is too much disparity in knowledge, the developer may become frustrated and eventually refuse to work with your person. Technical competency is critical in an effective QA organization. If you don't have the technical competence on your team for a project, you need to get busy doing training. Remember, technical competency doesn't necessarily mean you have to be coding in Java, but it might mean that you have to understand OO technology and terminology and be able to organize and execute an OO test project. And, as always, be sure you are technically competent as well.

Allow people to be responsible by encouraging ownership

If you just don't have enough people to match a QA person to a small set of developers, you can use functionality to assign the test team. You may also use skills and specialization (network experts, Unix system administrators, Windows test experts, etc.) to create your teams. I usually find it most advantageous to divide the work in the same way development has divided it, and then spread the specialized people (such as a Unix system administrator) across projects as a shared resource. Usually, software breaks down into areas or subsystems. By assigning the work by subsystem and setting up the bug tracking system in the same way, you have more efficiency and less unnecessary overlap between tasks. This allows you to define clear areas of responsibility, and people work better when they know they are responsible for an area. And, it is even better if they can retain this responsibility through maintenance releases and new feature releases. They will take ownership, and you will see improved work performance.

Proportion Allocation

One common trend in the industry is to determine the number of QA testers based upon the number of developers. This is usually done as a ratio, e.g., for every four developers there should be one QA person. In my sampling across a variety of software departments in a number of different industries, including commercial and government groups, the average ratio is 1:3, one QA person for every three developers. Some companies (notably some divisions within a really big software company in Redmond, WA) have a 1:1 ratio, and in some cases a 2:1 ratio where two QA people are assigned for each developer. The numbers vary widely throughout the industry.

Why use ratios to determine the size for the organization? It's easy. Management understands the formulas.[3] And generally, you can assume that a developer can turn out "x" amount of testable code, and that translates into needing "x" QA people to do adequate testing (assuming the quality is consistent), and that new code (as well as maintenance code) fit the same model. "Adequate testing" includes developing test cases and test documentation, conducting tests, developing and running automation, and conducting regression tests. Easy, right? Not quite. When calculating figures for your ratio, there are a few other items to consider.

---

3. Kathy Iberle (http://www.kiberle.com/articles.htm) elaborates on this topic in her article *Estimating Tester/Developer Ratios (or Not)*.

Number of platforms

Code may be developed on one platform and then ported. Testing must be done on all supported platforms, usually with the same amount of effort devoted to each. So, if your developer develops a Windows application on NT, and you have to test it on Win95, 98, 2K, ME, XP, and NT, this could severely mess up your numbers. If you figure that 40 hours of coding time equals 20 hours of testing time, for example, you're going to have to multiply those 20 hours times the number of platforms (or some factor if you don't do complete testing on all platforms).

Let's further expand this example. If you need to spend 20 hours to do 100% testing on NT, and also need to run 25% of the cases on Win95 and Win98, and 40% of the test cases on W2K, ME, and 80% on XP, you have the following time requirements:

Figure 13:
Testing across Platforms

Platform	% Test Cases	Hours Needed
NT	100%	20
Win95	25%	5
Win98	25%	5
Win2K	40%	8
ME	40%	8
XP	80%	16
Totals	310%	62 Hours

Your test time has now more than tripled! That makes for a significantly different estimate than if you were testing on just one platform.

Number of environments

Similar to the platform issue, the code may be developed with a certain set of compatibilities in mind. I worked for some time testing printer drivers. The developers would build the drivers to the specs of the printer, and subsequently release them to us to test. It was then our responsibility to see if the drivers worked with the 15 or so sample applications we had. Not only was this a lot of initial testing work, but when we found a bug, we then had to go back and see in which application environments the bug manifested itself. It's easy to see why that really big software company has to have such high ratios of testers. You can't release an operating system to the world without checking a lot of compatibilities – and that's the work of the testers, not the developers.

Localization testing

If you've never had to do localization testing on software that will be
released to the international market, consider yourself lucky. It's a lot of
work. Generally, the software is developed in English. Then it is sent somewhere to have all visible text translated into the supported languages (this
often includes multi-byte languages like Chinese, as well as the single-byte
European languages). Once translated, the software then arrives back at
your door to be tested. You realize how little you know about your software
when an error message appears in a language you can't read! Not only is
testing difficult, it is very time consuming. The developer will fix the bugs
– anomalies such as hard-coded strings that break functionality when
they're translated – but only after you notice and identify them. Depending
upon the number of languages, you may have 30 extra versions of the software to test. Also, remember that once you find a bug in the base code, you
will then have to retest all the rebuilt translated versions.

But I can't read Hebrew!

Design and Architecture Time

QA must be involved at these stages in the project. Early QA involvement
has been proven again and again to be the most cost effective way to produce quality software on or ahead of schedule. Let's look at an example:

If we're not involved in the design phases, we can't help build quality into the product

   How much does a bug cost a company if it gets to the field? That
depends on the bug and the customer, right? What if you're working on
software that reports readings from a medical device used in critical cases?
What if the readings are reported incorrectly? This could be catastrophic
for the company in terms of lawsuits, loss of good will, future business
potential … to say nothing of the patient. What if your company makes
software that determines how much ink a printer ejects, and there's a bug
that causes too much ink to be released? People will not be pleased with
their ink-covered desks and clothes. Is this a catastrophic bug? Probably
not, unless it happens to the person who is writing a review of the printer
for a national publication.

   So, what is the cost of a bug that makes it to the field? The only true
answer is, it depends. At a minimum, you have to consider the tangible
costs of your customer support infrastructure, the cost to document and
retest the problem (perhaps the cost to reconfigure the lab to do so), the
cost for the developer to fix it, the retest, and the release process to get
the fix out to the customers. Then there are the intangible costs of the

potential loss of future sales, goodwill, potential lawsuits, etc. This is potentially the most expensive, high-risk problem – the one that gets all the way to the customer who is negatively affected.

So, how much does a bug cost if it is caught in testing? Considerably less than one that gets to the field. You still have to pay for your testing infrastructure and bug tracking system, and the person hours to find it, report it, track it, fix it, and retest it. But, you save all those potentially catastrophic costs of a problem found in the field. The savings could be huge.

Bugs caught earlier are cheaper!

Better yet, what if the problem is caught by the developer during unit test or desk checking? Now you're not even taking any specific testing time for investigating the problem, reporting it, retesting the fix, or regression testing. Ideally, the developer still logs the problem in the bug tracking system so you can track the number and severity of the bugs found at this stage in the software lifecycle.

The best scenario is when bugs are caught in the design phase, before any effort has been expended to develop or test the code. Not only is this the least expensive place to find bugs, it's also the best place to find the big problems with the requirements. Have you ever successfully tested and released a product that didn't fulfill the customer's needs? This product will fail just as abysmally as one that's bug-ridden. Catch the design problems now, and save everyone time. This is the way to cut down on your testing time – ensure a stable design or a product that will fulfill the customer's needs.

Why is it cheaper and more efficient to find bugs earlier in the cycle? Because having fewer people involved and lower infrastructure costs result in lower product costs. Figure 14 shows a sample of some cost areas, and those that are affected based on when the bug is found and resolved. You can use this chart to add or delete affected areas and associated costs. If you determine that the average bug takes a developer an hour to investigate, you can assign a monetary value based on the developer's average salary. If you determine the average bug takes ten hours of testing time, you can figure out an average cost. Infrastructure costs need to be amortized over the expected bugs found (keeping in mind that fewer bugs will eventually require less infrastructure). Using the numbers that make sense to your company, you can see how the costs increase the longer the bug remains unresolved.

	Design	Development	Test	Post-Release
Design Analysis	X	X	X	X
Developer investigation		X	X	X
Bug Tracking System		X	X	X
Testing Time			X	X
Testing Infrastructure			X	X
Bug Tracking Effort			X	X
Release Process				X
Customer Support Infrastructure				X
Potential Loss of Sales				X
Potential Loss of Goodwill				X
Potential Lawsuits				X
Other Bad Stuff				X

Figure 14:
Cost Area Affected
Based on Phase
of Discovery/Resolution

The time to do the design reviews and monitor the unit testing doesn't come free, though. You must calculate it into your ratio figures. This is particularly important if non-coding personnel are used for the design/architecture steps. Be sure to account for the input of these people and your resulting participation.

Why is this involvement so critical to the success of the project? There are a number of reasons, including the following:

- Problems found earlier are cheaper to fix in terms of time and resources.
- QA input at this point in the project helps to find problems. The QA people who attend these reviews must have the requisite skills for the job. It's no help to send someone to a database design review if they don't know a column from a row.
- A quality presence at all the meetings helps keep quality consciousness and testability in the foreground.
- Early QA involvement facilitates intelligent manpower allocation. Skill sets can be aligned, and training needs can be assessed and addressed.
- Automation plans can be started now. An automation effort is a project in itself, and it can involve a significant amount of time and resources. By understanding the new software as early as possible, participating in

the requirements sessions, and acquiring an understanding of the intended use of the product, you will be able to make intelligent decisions regarding where to invest your automation resources. If the product will experience high user volumes, it is time to start planning the stress, load, and performance tests.

Stealth Projects

Are there other projects on which the developers may be spending some of their time? I have had my schedule and manpower allocation disrupted several times by "a really cool new program that Bob's been working on in the evenings" that has somehow found its way into the product. Keep an eye on anyone, particularly Bob, who is working on special projects that may be generating some unexpected work for you.

Support

Anytime I've released a new product, my group has been involved in supporting it. Sometimes this meant working with and training the support people. Sometimes this meant answering the phones when beta customers called. Sometimes it meant going on site. This can be a significant time drain in a project, and it is a time drain that development doesn't experience. If this is likely to happen to you, you should also be aware of the potential morale and skills issues. Some people don't want to do support. Some can't, due to their inability to present the helpful support persona. Before you get pulled into the morass of support, be sure you have a way to get back out of it eventually.

Unscheduled, Emergency Releases

Creating a release takes QA time, and a good part of that is overhead, not testing. If you have extra releases to create, you need to factor that time into your ratio. Creating a release usually requires significantly more QA effort than development effort. Development may review your release notes, but that doesn't take nearly as much time as it does to gather and create the notes in the first place, prepare the media, test the final versions, and so on.

Sales Situations

Do you need to worry that your people will have to test prototype, pre-release software? Is it possible that you may need to send people to support the sales staff with new products? Or go to trade shows to make sure Marketing doesn't embarrass the company? I've been in all these situations. Development resources weren't used for these instances, because we in QA had a better understanding of how to make the product work by tiptoeing through the tulip field that was littered with bugs.

Flow of Work

One final issue when looking at proportion allocation: will there be a steady flow of work? I've worked on several projects where I had the right number of people, and we were busily working along when suddenly there was a disruption in the flow of new code to us. We had adequately tested what we had previously been given, then we were suddenly faced with a couple weeks with nothing to do. We were right on schedule (that should have warned me right there that something was wrong!), so the test cases were current.

These disruptions often happen in the best-run projects. You may have an unexpected holdup from a third party. In my case, we were stalled while waiting on new versions of firmware that would cause significant development changes to the code. Be sure you are planning for these slow times. It is a good idea to make sure you have background projects for people to move to in these situations. I like to have several non-critical automation projects available just in case. These kinds of projects provide a good learning environment, produce useful products, and maintain the momentum. You sure don't want to have a group of people sitting around with nothing better to do than surf the web – it can easily become a habit that is hard to break when the work picks up again.

As part of the requirements and design phases, you should also be on the lookout for these types of down periods. Sometimes these down periods can be eliminated by rearranging the order in which the software to be tested arrives in QA. It is important to work with development at the early stages of the project to be sure the release schedule works for both groups.

Not Enough Bodies

More bodies often equals
more problems

In the grand scheme of project management, it is sometimes well recognized that the testing load is too high to release the product by the target date with an adequate level of quality. Bravo! In this case, we'd like to see a phased release of the software, earlier QA involvement in the development lifecycle to allow more efficient testing with fewer bugs, and a tightly coupled development/test effort. Hah! Silly us. Unfortunately, the answer that seems obvious to management is to throw more bodies at the problem. Untrained bodies. And guess who is going to be responsible for training them, overseeing them, and ensuring the quality of their work is acceptable? That's right, you're the one who wanted that management position.

There are generally three ways in which bodies are hurriedly added to QA: have the developers do testing, pay for contractors, or outsource some or all of the testing. What can you expect to happen in each of these scenarios (other than the recurrence of your drinking problem)?

When Developers Test

Developers don't approach software in the same way that QA people do. While they may intimately know their code, they may not know the surrounding code and may not know the intended use of the code. Good developers will do good unit testing, and that's what they should do. When developers are brought in to help QA, there is generally some resentment on their part because they don't really want to be doing QA work. They want to be doing development. I've had good luck using developers to work with my automation people. I've had good luck getting developers to spend a day or so testing someone else's code. I've not had success with having developers assigned to me for testing purposes for extended periods of time – the skill sets and interests just are not the same.

If developers are assigned
to testing, be sure you can
audit their results

Unfortunately, if you go to management with your well-conceived test plan and your prioritized risk analysis, and clearly make a case that more time is needed to release software with the agreed-upon level of quality, management will likely propose a solution. Assigning developers to you might be that solution. So now what? If you refuse, you're being uncooperative. If you accept, you know you're in for a lot of oversight work without commensurate rewards. Make a counter offer. Ask if the developers would create an automated suite of unit tests with verifiable results. Ask them to create and document test cases – this will be a good opportunity to see where they think their own code is weak. They will probably rebel against this task, which may help your case for getting qualified test people.

If you have to use developers due to time requirements, be sure you give them documented test cases that they have to sign off on. In this way, if they're responsible, they'll tend to take the work more seriously and will approach it with a more disciplined attitude. If they're lackadaisical about it, at least you'll have evidence of what they claimed to have tested when quality problems surface in the field. It won't help you right now, but it may help next time you are offered "assistance." Allowing developers to do only ad hoc testing will offer no measurable gain for you and will likely cause you extra time in supporting them. Some of my more negative colleagues have suggested that having developers test is akin to trying to teach a pig to sing. It doesn't work and it annoys the pig.

When Contractors Arrive on Your Doorstep

Contractors can be used effectively, but keep in mind that you have to train them. If you're going to use contractors, be sure you'll be able to retain them for at least twice the amount of time it takes you to train them. If a contractor requires three months of training, be sure the contract is for at least six months. Assume it will take 1/3 of a person to train and oversee the work of a contractor. Therefore, adding three contractors to your testing herd results in a net gain of three newly trained people after the training period is complete and the loss of one experienced person during the training period. It is an expensive way to proceed, but you may have no choice. Be sure that your management understands the cost of training.

This is a big consideration if you're thinking about staffing to your schedule's valleys and using contractors to handle the peaks. In my experience, unless those peaks are more akin to plateaus, you'll be wasting a lot of training and management time with little quality testing in return.

We'll Just Outsource Some Work

Outsourcing work seems like a great idea, doesn't it? You can get rid of some of the monotonous work that no one wants to do anyway. That will work well for you as long as you can supply the outsource group with all the information, equipment, and software they need to do the work

Is outsourcing the latest silver bullet?

independently. And that's assuming you have a reliable way to regularly assess their progress. Even in this ideal situation, you will need to find the outsource group, devise the contract, verify that their estimates are realistic, oversee the work, and have a means to verify the results of their work. That takes a significant amount of a senior person's time.

If your product does not lend itself to independent testing, you will need to be ready to support the outsource group at a higher level than your own people. Remember, these people aren't as familiar with your software and environment as you are. More importantly, they are probably charging you by the hour even if they are sitting there for an hour waiting for you to get them unstuck. Be sure your outsource group has adequate system administration support.

Offshore outsourcing is a common panacea these days. We've all heard how inexpensive it is to have work done abroad. That's fine if the group is as well trained as your people, is as disciplined and responsible as your people, and has everything they need to work effectively and independently. If you have support issues with the offshore folks, you have the added burden of time and language differences. If you must go offshore with some of the testing, be sure it's very independent code. Highly integrated code needs to be tested in a single location. The logistical problems introduced with a geographically dispersed testing effort often will eliminate any anticipated cost reductions. You will also need to consider the coordination issues, particularly if you work in a very dynamic, changing environment with little structure or documentation. It is extremely difficult to coordinate with people who are never in the office at the same time as your team.

Outsourcing may not be an inexpensive alternative

In any outsource testing project, ownership of the test cases and test plans must be made clear. Who will make changes? Who will post results to your test management system? Will your bug tracking system be open to the outsource group? Are there security issues in exposing your known bugs to a third party? How will configuration management work? How do new releases of software get to the outsource group? How good does the code need to be before it gets sent to the outsource group? All these questions must be answered and the required time estimated before the outsourcing decision can be made. These are all costs which will occur in the outsource project. The hourly rate of the outsource company is only one consideration. As a rule of thumb, I expect to allocate one of my people full-time for every five to seven people supplied by the outsource company.

6 Keeping Your Beast Effective

You can hire and build a first class team, but you have to work to keep that team effective. In this section we're going to explore techniques to master productive communication, and ways to determine the optimal composition of your teams. We'll also examine what is at the root of an effective team, and how to use those roots as the foundation on which your team can grow.

Master Effective Communication

Communication generally goes in three directions: up, down, or sideways. In order to effectively communicate, you must be able to take information from any direction and send it out in any direction.

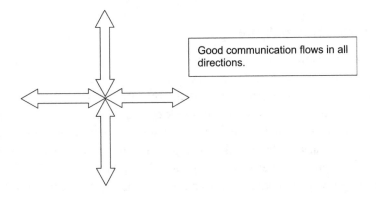

Good communication flows in all directions.

Figure 15:
Communication Flow

Sounds simple? Not so. Before you set out to be the company's best communicator, be sure you are thinking about three things:

- What is the content of the message, and how is it likely to be received?
- Who needs to know this information, and who does not need to know?
- What is the best way to communicate the information?

Inward Communication

Everyone interprets information in terms of how it affects them

Let's take an example. You've just been told that a major contract has been signed. This is good news. Everyone will be happy to hear this, right? Maybe – maybe not. Remember, people are most interested in how the information affects them personally. As a manager, you may have a more global perspective. Or, you may also be thinking in terms of how this news will affect your own job. A new contract has been signed, which means guaranteed work for the next year. No layoffs! That's great news to you as a manager, and you're sure your people will also be happy.

But, what if they weren't even thinking about layoffs? What if their major concern has to do with too big a workload and the number of hours they will have to work to take on this new project? Theirs is a completely different perspective. While you think you have only good news to convey, remember your audience. They may have other concerns. It is always best to try to anticipate these concerns and address them when you present information. Let's face it though. There are a lot of concerns that you will not think about. In this case you need to be sure you provide adequate time, and an open environment for these concerns to be aired and addressed.

Remember Your Audience

Downward communication can be tricky. The most important thing to consider is how your audience will receive the information. When you present any kind of information, particularly if it's unexpected, people will be looking to you to see what you think of it. Your enthusiasm with the new contract will help to convince them that you're presenting good news. If you stutter around for a while and express the information with concern about schedules and headcount, that's how it will be received. This is the time to show your maturity and present the information positively and honestly. You will always have concerns about any news, but you don't need to make those concerns public unless it is the correct time to let people know they should be worried too.

There are also cases when you receive information from your management that shouldn't be passed down the chain. That's part of your job, too. While you're always loyal to your people, there are often confidential issues that belong at your level and no lower. Let's say you were just told the quarter revenues of your publicly traded company are significantly below estimates. Layoffs were discussed as a means of reducing expenses. Should you tell your people? Probably not yet. If you're not sure, ask your boss. Respect information like this.

Open Doors

What about incoming communication? You want to be sure each one of your people has a communication path to you. You can do this via the fabled "open door policy," but that is often a term used by people who are notorious for keeping their doors the very opposite of open. I have found that people are much more reluctant to bring an item (particularly a problem item) to me in my office than they are to spill it out when I'm sitting next to them in the lab. The casual environment is more comfortable.

My door is always open, unless it's closed

If one of your people is having a problem with a developer, by the time they come into your office to tell you about it, it's really a big problem. If, on the other hand, you are available in a more casual environment; in their cubical/office, in the lab, or in the coffee room, they will feel more free to talk to you and will bring up the subject much sooner. This allows you to address the problem situation before it escalates. Think about it. If you're taking a problem to your boss, the formal office environment is equal to making a formal complaint. Gee, it really isn't that bad; maybe you'll just let it wait for a while …

Don't Overreact!

One very important thing to consider is how you're going to react to information you receive. Sometimes people just want to complain and don't want any particular action from you. Everybody needs to blow off steam now and then. I much prefer that they do that with me than to everyone they meet in the hallway. I often ask people what they'd like me to do about the situation. Often the answer is, "Well, actually I don't want you to do anything yet. I just wanted you to be aware of the problem." Great. I can do that. Now I know there's a potential issue so I can keep an eye on the problem, and they know I am there to help if the situation doesn't get rectified.

You do not want to be the person no one talks to because you'll overreact to a situation. I worked with a CEO who felt it was his duty to react (more like blow up) over any issue that came to his attention. It reached the point where the guys wouldn't even go in the bathroom if he was in there for fear he'd ask how things were going. That's not the environment you want to accidentally create.

Outward Communication

Show support without showing distrust

Outward communication is also an area you need to monitor. If you have project leads working for you, can you trust them to go to the project meetings to represent your department? Can they handle a barrage of questions if the project is having schedule or budget problems? You want to be available to back up your leads in tricky situations. If you think the lead is likely to attract unfriendly fire in a meeting, you may want to go with them. Explain why you're going so they don't think it is because you don't trust them. It's often a good idea to review what will be presented, and ask if they'd like you to go with them. That shows your support without giving the impression of distrust.

Generally, anything above project level communication should go through you. That way you can be sure your department is presenting a consistent face to the world, and that policies and procedures which are implemented will work across all projects. If you're going into a policy discussion that directly affects only one project but has far-reaching implications, include your project lead in the meeting too. They will learn about policy decisions, they'll be able to apply the decisions to their project, and they'll see the other factors that have to be considered regarding other projects. Remember, the faster you train your leads to handle more issues, the sooner you can spend your days sitting with your feet on your desk.

Beware of the Grapevine

Respect and never, ever underestimate the grapevine

Don't forget about all-powerful casual communication, sometimes known as the grapevine. People talk. Sometimes, one of the unfortunate byproducts of getting cross-functional teams working together is that they will also talk about "stuff". Work stuff. All the better, you think? But what if you had just discovered a catastrophic bug late in the testing cycle and you're working on how to present it to your management. You really wouldn't want them to find out about it via your person who found the bug, who told their buddy in support, who told their manager, who blew up because it is the same type of bug that occurred in the last release. This incensed manager then called your manager, who was completely blind-sided. Yow!

This stuff happens. Believe me though, the last thing you want to do is put a gag order on people. That usually has two negative byproducts. One, they talk about the gag order, immediately identifying you as the withholder of information; and two, they still talk about what they're not supposed to – because now it is more fun. It's much better to get word to your management as quickly as possible if something bad has happened, because nothing remains a secret for long in any organization. The good part about the grapevine is that sometimes you'll receive information more quickly this way than you would through formal channels. Respect the grapevine; use it when you need to, yet beware of it at the same time.

Creating Optimal Project Teams

In order to create optimal teams, we have to know a few things. How many teams will we need? Who can lead those teams? Leads should lead, but many do not. You need to train them how to do it, and then let them try it.

What is the most efficient structure within the organization? Any sizable department will contain subdivisions – official or not. These subdivisions, or project teams, need to be formed because they are needed for real work. You want to be sure that the team structure facilitates doing the work. Don't try to fit the work into the structure. It will help you later if you don't make false project divisions just because you have idle leads.

Figure 16:

Sample Project Teams

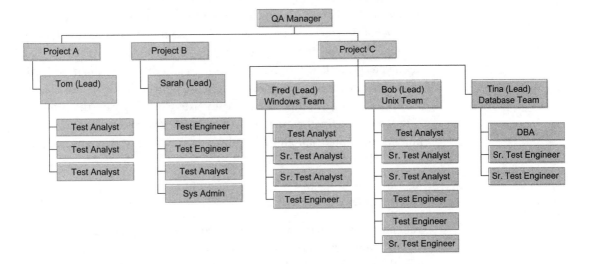

If we look at the example of a department with several projects, we can see various ways to partition the work. For Project A and B, we need single teams, each with a lead. Project C is much bigger and more diverse. In this case, I have leads handling the different technologies within the project. I might also want to have one lead in charge of the entire project, or, as in this case, I'm going to manage it myself. There is a lot of flexibility in how to create your project teams. You have to work with the projects and people that you have, trying to match the skills with the opportunities.

When promoting leads, it is beneficial to make clear that a lead position is transitive depending on the project allocations. By defining the lead position as an opportunity position, you've built maximum flexibility into your team. As projects and subprojects come and go, you can apply your leads effectively – matching skills and experience to best meet the goals of your company. It also can help with inflated ego problems if your leads know they may be a lead on this project, but they may be a senior tester working under another lead on the next project.

How Many Teams Do You Need?

Defining how many teams are required is one of the most difficult and critical tasks you will face as a manager. A wrong decision here will descend you into the hell of projects running amuck, unmotivated and ineffective people, and unhappiness which may lead to mutiny within the organization. What do you need to consider when making project teams? First of all, how many distinct projects do you have? Distinct projects can be defined as projects with different deadlines and different human or hardware/software resources. How long do these projects last? Or, more realistically, how long are they scheduled to last? How "big" are the projects? "Big" can be defined as the amount of code, number of configurations, number of people, amount of equipment, schedule, and relative importance of the project.

The Art of Delegation

You may have clearly defined and sized projects, but before you put together your project teams you need to be sure you will have someone to lead them. Are your leads capable of taking over a project team or two? Can you effectively delegate to your leads? To know this, you need to think about your comfort level. What does your personal involvement need to be? You may have someone you can delegate work to, and you may be comfortable in doing so. But, there may be an expectation within the project team that you will be personally involved. And what do you do in this case? Delegate. And go to whatever project meetings you need to attend until the comfort level with the new lead is established. You owe them the opportunity.

Creative Team Organization

Once you have answered these questions, you'll know how many project teams you need and how many you can create. Unfortunately, those numbers won't necessarily match, but that's reality. It is still good to know how many project teams you should have, even if you can't make that many because you don't have enough people or equipment or leaders. In addition to the project method for creating teams, you may also have some service-oriented teams who assist across projects. These may include performance specialists, domain experts, and utility testers who hop from project to project based on workload. Maintaining flexibility is one of the most important aspects to consider when creating your teams.

Be sure each individual is adequately managed

When you are creating your organizations within your organization, be sure that each individual in your group will be adequately managed – receiving enough attention to meet their needs and yours. Ensure that the information flow is streamlined for efficiency. Too many levels of hierarchy result in too many chiefs in too many meetings. Your ample quantity of chiefs may find the need to create more meetings to justify their existence.

Be sure your group has the right number of leaders, and that the right people are assigned to them. This means you have to know your leads before you assign people to them. You can have a great engineer and a great lead, but they might not be good together – one could be a very independent worker, while the other could be a very hands-on worker. Our industry has sometimes created environments where the prima donna is allowed to flourish. You'll want to be careful not to let this mindset fester in your organization, or you will be setting yourself up for some long term problems. So, while it is only intelligent to try to group people into effective groups where they are comfortable, don't cripple your organization by catering to problematic individuals with unreasonable wants. Professionals

More leaders may equal more meetings

should work together professionally, and sometimes they need to be reminded.

Let Your Leads Lead

Allow your lead to evolve   As mentioned earlier, I assume a lead will have some role in personnel management. You may want that responsibility to evolve over time. If your lead is new or inexperienced, consider giving them project responsibility without personnel responsibility. This provides a good training ground with less risk. People are more amenable to a team assignment if their administrative manager is not changed. As soon as administrative reporting is changed, people become concerned about their performance review and their career plans. By not changing administrative reporting, you can supply continuity in their career growth plans while allowing your people to work on a variety of projects.

Allow your lead to grow into the role. The transition will occur naturally if the ability is there. There will be less anxiety for the team members if the leader is not forced upon them. By easing in the transition there is less anxiety for the lead, and they won't have to face undeserved opposition. People tend to resist change. Try not to force your lead into that resistance. Conversely, the lead may also feel insecure in the new position. This sometimes results in their demanding more authority and control; a demand that immediately causes resentment, which in turn makes them feel more insecure. By creating a safe environment for the lead where they are accepted, you have launched them into the opportunity in the best possible way.

What happens if you have an accelerated schedule, and you need a lead for a project right now? You don't have time to let the lead evolve into the position. Reality is such a pain, isn't it? You need to accelerate the lead's acceptance. You can do this by trying not to immediately assign personnel responsibility, thus working around the possible resistance that people may have to the change in administrative reporting. Give your lead opportunities to build rapport. Let them bring in the bagels each week. Let them tell people good news about the project. You can also help your lead succeed by making sure the schedule and manpower allocation is correct. If there's bad news to deliver to the team, do it yourself. Don't make the lead be the bad guy, and don't put them in a position where they have to defend you – that's tricky stuff which has to wait until they have more practice.

Most importantly, stay close to your leads. Support them, and don't let them fail. If they fail, so do you.

Back to Our Roots

What is at the root of an effective team?

- People know what they're doing – they have the technical capabilities and people skills necessary to get the job done effectively.
- People enjoy what they're doing – people like to come to work each day and are enjoying their daily tasks and their overall project assignments.
- People want to do what they are assigned to do – they feel that their current tasks are what they should be doing. Their career is advancing according to their plans, and their work is facilitating their long-term goals. This is discussed in depth in Chapter 11 – Growing Your Staff.
- There is no internal strife – the members of your department get along.
- Life is wonderful, and the entire company gets along… – hey, it might happen!

Well, maybe not the last one, but certainly the first four are factors that will make for an effective team for a long time. Write these down and stick them on your office wall. You will want to refer back to this list when the schedules explode and/or people quit. Remember, if you ever get to the place where each of these items holds true, you can sit all day with your feet on your desk and count the ceiling tiles.

7   Creating Synergy and Pride

We Love Us, Why Doesn't Everyone Else?

It's time to be honest here. QA is often considered a necessary evil. This isn't exactly the description we were hoping for when we took the job. I bet you didn't go to college and look at the career center postings thinking, "Ah, Necessary Evil, that's what I want to be." On the other hand, the "necessary" part is a good thing. QA has to be recognized as necessary. Once you've hurdled that obstacle, you can fix the evil (unless of course you like being referred to as evil, in which case you might want to consider a different career – we don't need you cluttering up the world of QA).

Emphasize the Necessary

How do you make sure your department is considered to be necessary? By providing a tangible product. Remember, you may be competing for funding and headcount with development. If the VP of Engineering has money to spend, how will he decide? If he spends it on development, he'll get this cool new program that does stuff. If he spends it on QA he'll get … what exactly? More bugs identified? Well, what good is that? You need to be sure your department is producing a tangible product that can be understood and described to your management. Did you already do the test plans? Great. You probably also keep track of the test cases, and the bugs you find. But what does that mean to your management when they are thinking about spending money on you? Can you guarantee to your boss that if he gives you two more people, you will find 500 more bugs and make the product safe for humanity? No. But the development manager can promise that two more people will result in two more cool programs that can be seen, demonstrated, and sold for revenue.

Determining ROI (Return on Investment) for QA

This has always been a quandary for us in QA, and particularly for QA management. For all the years I've done QA management work, this has been one of the most difficult aspects of the job. Fortunately there is a good way to track and project what the QA group will accomplish, and how additional resources will affect the outcome of the goals. I'm a strong advocate of approaching quality assurance as a risk management function. Given any project (of any size), you first define the risks that you are trying to mitigate. What are all the bad things that could happen if this software doesn't work? It is a scary thought, isn't it? But that's where you start.

Clarify your goals and contributions

For example, what happens if the software will not install? That is bad: a high priority risk that must be mitigated. Is it something you can catch in testing? Yes. Can you build a test case or a suite of test cases to check for this problem? Yes. By creating a risk analysis and a mitigation strategy (testing and quality assurance), you are able to present a picture that management will understand. You can offer a giant list of all the risks inherent in this software. You can offer a list of all the things we can do to mitigate the risks. And you can explain how long it will take to carry them out. This can mean executing test cases, participating in design reviews, or even verifying the documentation. Each action requires time and resources. If you have a limited amount of time and resources, you can draw an accurate picture of how much risk mitigation you can offer.

It is important to emphasize that your department's goal is not to find and report bugs, but rather to provide a risk management system that will help deliver a higher quality product to your customers. For more information regarding how to build and maintain this approach, see Rex Black's book: *Managing the Testing Process*.

But They Still Think We're Evil!

We will assume you've established that your department is a necessary cog in the corporate machine. Now we have to dispel the evil aura that sometimes surrounds the QA group. Our industry is not immune to the occasional bad apple. I personally have met some really obnoxious QA people with whom I had absolutely no desire to work with. I pity their developers. In the QA world (and more often than in other technical fields), diplomacy is a requirement. As was discussed in the section on interviewing and hiring, you have to start with people who can do their job and who can work effectively with others. Still, even with a group of technically sound and diplomatic folks, there is sometimes the predisposition among developers to judge QA as evil.

Problem Solver or Problem Causer?

The good news is that there is one thing you personally can do to help improve your department's reputation. You must always be perceived as part of the team that will solve the project problems. This isn't an easy role, because you are often in the position of pointing the project problems out in the first place. Everyone in management knows it is better to be presented with a problem *and* a solution, rather than just a problem and shrugged shoulders. So, think about it. Let's say the schedule is in the tank. What can you do?

First of all, meet with the development manager and see if he has any ideas. He may be the reason your project is in trouble, so perhaps he has thought of ways to get it back out of trouble. If that doesn't work, get out your carefully prepared risk analysis. You were planning on testing 75% of the high-risk items. Now you may only have time for 50%. Do you simply move the cutoff line up the chart and get back to work? Probably not. One of the common mistakes we make in QA management is taking ownership of a problem that isn't ours. So, now our schedule is in trouble, but not as a result of testing issues. What do we do next?

Don't take ownership of a problem that isn't yours

This isn't a decision you can make. It is time to reconvene the project group (including project management and development), and get an opinion. This is objective data, so you can treat it as such. "Here's the plan, here's where we are. We could test just to this point, but I'm worried that we'll leave these important areas untouched." It may be that you can reorganize the priorities, and get a wider range of testing done at a higher level. This might be safer in the long run, depending upon the product. The actual approach you settle on will vary by project. The important thing is that you're working integrally as a part of the project team to find a solution to the problem. It's not just your problem; it is the team's problem. By getting the entire team involved, ownership becomes shared (and, negatively speaking, the blame is also shared), proper exposure is given, and a more creative solution may be possible.

Unrealistic Expectations

If expectations are unrealistic, who set them?

As a manager or lead, you may find yourself defending your group against someone's unrealistic expectations. That's never a comfortable position, but if you find yourself in it, you need to figure out how those unreasonable expectations got set in the first place. Did you fail to do adequate project preparation, making clear how the testing would be executed? Did they expect the performance problems to be found at the beginning of testing, before you had adequate functionality to run the load tests? Anytime you find yourself on the defensive, you should be able to point to documentation that was previously presented that explains your position. If you don't have that documentation, maybe you didn't do your job in the project planning stages. Now you know what to improve upon next time.

The same applies if you find yourself giving anything but an objective response with supporting data. The only reason to be giving an emotional or off-the-cuff response to project issues, is that you didn't do the planning and gather the documentation you needed to support yourself. Have you ever been asked how you know a product is ready to ship? The correct answer is not, "Because it feels right." The correct answer is demonstrated in charts and graphs showing the risks that were mitigated by the successful execution of the specified test cases. Since (after reading this) you will be doing excellent planning and documenting, remember to regularly publish your progress documents so issues can be raised early.

Presenting Your Information

I worked with a QA manager who had been backed into a corner by a project that was on fire. The development manager had been telling the executive staff that the project was on schedule. The QA manager had not wanted to contradict the development manager in a meeting, but clearly there were still glitches in the software. After much discussion with him, it became apparent that the plan still called for the software to be delivered on schedule, but not in such an order that allowed any functional testing to take place. This was a huge problem. The development manager could honestly say that he had delivered 90% of the software to QA, but the vast majority of the software was not testable because the missing 10% provided the communication between the UI (user interface) and the database back-end processes.

We worked out a way to present the data clearly and accurately to our management, and got the development manager to agree that it was an accurate representation. We took the development manager's original slide that showed the percent of software delivered by subsystem, and added a column indicating how much of each subsystem was testable, and another column indicating how much had actually been tested. The chart looked like the following:

Subsystem	% delivered to QA	% testable	% tested
SubsystemA	90	25	20
SubsystemB	85	30	25
SubsystemC	95	10	5
SubsystemD	100	15	0
Average:	92.5	20	12.5

Figure 17:
Bad News

This gave quite a different picture to management; not a happy picture, but one they could clearly understand, which was our goal. We had the data and were able to present it objectively. Now everyone understood that we had a problem project, and we could work together on a solution. It was also vitally important that the development manager agreed with our data. When we presented this information, he was the first one to be questioned about its veracity. Fortunately, he was honest. He was also an excellent developer and manager. We were lucky.

What if he hadn't been willing to share the blame and acknowledge the problem? We had documentation for that too. We were prepared to show the detailed risk analysis, which showed the prioritization of our test cases. In our risk analysis, we had highlighted which risks we had been able to mitigate – a pitifully small number. We also had the list of all the necessary test cases and which ones we could actually execute. Knowing that this would bore our non-technical executive team, we picked out a few selected cases that showed the glaring lack of functionality. All of this documentation supported our information (which, by the way, was correct and unembellished).

These kinds of situations highlight the importance of working with the development team and the development manager, right from the start of the project. If you don't have a solid relationship built on honesty, this kind of crisis will escalate. If you present your data and the development team debates it, you can haul out all your backup information (as we were

Present a united front with development

prepared to do), although management is still left with the uncomfortable impression of internal quarrels and unnecessary impediments to getting the work done. If development is favored in your work environment, you are likely to be the recipient of the blame for the problems of not being able to "work together."

This is an unfortunate reality in many organizations. The only way to fix it is to build a positive relationship from the beginning, so you are always working together on the project with the developers. This is easy to say, but hard to do. Unfortunately, you can be technically sound and absolutely correct with all your information, yet still find yourself in one of these situations where the development group has managed to cloud the water with enough squid ink that no one is sure who is at fault. Uh-oh. It is best not to infuriate the squid. Work with him, and make him work with you throughout the project.

Job Satisfaction

That's right, we're cool. But sometimes, even with all the correct planning and documentation, a product ships before it should. I worked in one company that was completely driven by hardware schedules. When the hardware was ready, the accompanying software shipped, regardless of its quality. And, to make matters worse, my division only did the initial software release. Another company did all subsequent maintenance releases, so we never got to see any product improvements over time.

Pride and Ownership

Good QA people want to deliver good products. The more ownership of a product or subsystem of a product they feel, the more they care about its quality. Part of their job satisfaction comes from knowing they did a good job managing the risks of the product and saving the customer from the horrors that the previously buggy software would have caused. Unfortunately, that's not really what the job is. As a manager, you need to make clear to your people what the job is not. It is not to ensure that the software has no bugs when it gets to the customer. It is not to ensure that the software is the coolest stuff on the market. It is not to ensure that every release will be shipped on time, and will be a stunning success in the field.

So what is the job? The job is to execute all the scheduled test cases to mitigate the priority risks. And, yes; you also want to find and document bugs, and accurately identify and classify those bugs. The job is to make a summary appraisal on the quality of the software by evaluating the risks. And, probably most importantly, the job is to provide factual information to the decision makers. This can be a very different picture from the expectations your people may have for their jobs, and the areas from which they expect to gain job satisfaction.

Our job is to provide factual information to the decision makers

Risk Mitigation

Personally, I love to find bugs – the more complicated and elusive the better. That is what satisfies me. I am downright unhappy if I run a bunch of test cases and don't find any defects. If my test cases don't find bugs, does that mean I'm not doing a good job? Not at all. My job is to mitigate risks, not find bugs. The fact that I ran the test cases means I mitigated the risks those cases cover. You want to orient your group so that they are driven to mitigate risks, not find bugs. If the goal is to find bugs (or worse), and if evaluation is based on the number of bugs found, what happens if you get stuck testing software that's very solid and works well? We spend a lot of time testing things that work (we hope!).

You want to be sure you get the credit for all the time spent, not just the time that resulted in bug detection. Be sure to publish the test case execution results, and the risk mitigation results along with your bug reports. Upper management is often fixated on bugs found rather than risks mitigated, and these are very different results from the testing effort. Spend the time to train your management so they understand the goals. In this way you can reinforce those goals with your people, and increase their job satisfaction when they have completed test cases (whether or not bugs were found).

Ship It!

It's your job to constantly remind people that they don't have to agree with the decision to ship, but they are expected to provide accurate information. They don't have to fix the bugs, they just identify and classify them correctly. They don't need to take on a personal crusade for the quality of the software. If you can get these messages across to your group, they will be happier in their jobs, and will enjoy their contribution to their projects.

Those who like what they do will do a better job, work harder at it, learn what they need to know on their own time, and will make their own rewards. You can't control someone else's job satisfaction, but you can provide an environment which will allow them to glean what they need.

Synergy, Pride, and Celebration

Celebrate the little victories   As you rise higher in management, it can be easy to forget to celebrate the little victories. You move from one project to the next; as soon as one project is past the crisis stage, you're on to planning the next one (the next project, not the next crisis!). It is all too common to forget to celebrate the completion of the previous project before turning to the next one. Don't forget. Just because your own reward system may have changed, you still have people who were fixated on a project for some amount of time. They need to celebrate the successful completion – have a party!

Creating synergy and pride within your department is your job. Be a leader! How much does it mean to you to get a pat on the back? Remember, as you go higher, there are fewer tangible rewards. (On the day I received a promotion, a friend rudely pointed out to me the higher up the tree the monkey goes, the more of what is seen is the monkey's behind.) Just because you don't get them, doesn't mean you shouldn't give them. Be sure you recognize successes, and the effects of those successes. Your group may have just facilitated an early launch of a highly competitive product. They may not know that they were part of a project that just snuffed out the competition. Tell them! Celebrate the victories. Acknowledge and console when there are defeats as well. My department was once involved with a software release that never should have happened. It shipped (to our horror) on the scheduled date, despite the overwhelming evidence we presented. We knew the product would fail in the field, but we had done our job and supplied accurate information to the decision makers. Even though we felt rotten about the product, we had a project-completion luncheon anyway. We needed to spend a little time collectively as a group to discuss the business reasons why the decision to ship the product had been made, and I needed to remind everyone that we had done the job we were supposed to do. Everyone left the lunch feeling better about the work they'd done, and were energized to tackle the next project.

Never miss a chance to celebrate together as a group. Bring in donuts for hard days and nights. Give time off for extra hours spent. Treat people as if you are grateful for the work they've done, and the commitment they've shown. Remember, you are only as successful as your team makes you, so create genuine rewards for genuine effort. The little things do matter, so remember to say thank you, and send a nice email now and then. Food is always appreciated, so take people to lunch or buy them bagels for breakfast. Make people glad they work for you.

Deflecting Criticism and Building Respect

You have to defend your department from internal and external forces. You may find yourself in the role of deflecting criticism. QA generally receives a lot of criticism, and that is partly because we generate a lot of criticism. Isn't that what identifying a bug is? We can say that it's documentation of aberrant behavior, but to the developer, it is a criticism of their work. Frustration can run very high with developers, particularly when schedules are tight and bad bugs are found late in the process. Sometimes this will cause them to lash out, to you or to their management. So, what can be done to prevent hard feelings? As we've discussed in previous sections, a well-planned and well-documented test process will help relieve the frustration and finger pointing when the schedule blows up. Everyone will have already seen and agreed to the plan. You may not be able to follow that plan, but now you are completely within your rights to discuss any deviations with the stakeholders in the project. You're part of the team that will provide the solution to the problem; you're not the problem.

You're part of the team that will provide the solution to the project's problems

But What About Internal Problems?

In addition to deflecting criticism from outside your group, be sure your team does not explode from internal combustion. If you have problems brewing within (and you usually will), be sure you're constantly working to alleviate them. It is always best to learn about an internal problem from internal sources, but sometimes things boil over when you're not around. Be sure to listen! People need to feel free to talk to you or they won't bring you problems. If you're hearing about internal problems from external sources, you have communication issues in your department that need to be solved.

Be sure your group knows they can count on you. You need to be ready and able to act appropriately when faced with a personnel issue. If you criticize your group members to other people, they will find out and their trust in you will be destroyed. If you criticize group members to other group members, you should be shot. Well, maybe that's a little strong, but you get the point. There is no excuse for a manager to criticize one's peers. It makes everyone uncomfortable and destroys trust. The worst manager I've ever worked with criticized his people to non-management and management people, within and outside his department. Usually, a group with a bad manager will tend to band together against him. This is one of the least effective team building strategies! In the case of this manager of mine, he created so much distrust between the team members that they hated him AND they distrusted each other. It became the most dysfunctional group I've ever had the misfortune with which to work. Don't confide in others inappropriately. If you need to talk about an employee, find another manager at your level. Or get a dog – they can always be trusted to keep your confidences.

If you do decide to confide in another manager regarding your personnel problems, be sure you have an action plan. Don't just whine. If you're asking for advice, do so. But be prepared to act on that advice or explain why you won't. You don't want to appear weak and unable to deal with an employee problem. Be professional and think about what you want to gain from the discussion before you have it.

Remember to Remain Objective and Honest

When someone brings you an internal issue, what should you do? You want them to confide in you, but you don't want to give the appearance that you are agreeing with them. At this point, you need to be objective. You'll have to check the data to see if what you were told is valid, and determine if action is needed. Be very careful what you say, as it is likely to be repeated. If someone comes in your office and says, "I hate working with Joe; he's always such a grump in the morning," don't nod your head and say, "Yeah, I noticed." You can bet as soon as your complainer leaves the office, the whole group will know you said Joe's a grump in the morning, and you hate working with him. Depending on the speed of your grapevine, you can probably count on a visit from Joe before lunch, and he definitely will be grumpy!

When someone does bring a problem to you, be sure you are honest with them. Be sure they leave your office confident that they have given you information and you will act appropriately. This doesn't mean to encourage tattling. The last thing you want is to be resolving every little personnel issue that occurs. You are paying people adult wages and they should act like adults. At least that is what I keep telling myself. There is nothing wrong with sending someone from your office with the advice that maybe they need to work out the problem on their own, and they should come back if there are further issues.

You need to be sure that you have people in your department who will be honest with you, even with something you don't want to hear. I once made a presentation to my department in which I discussed a job classification change that affected the Senior Engineer requirements. Unfortunately, during the presentation, I misspoke and said Engineer instead of Senior Engineer. That would have made almost all the Engineers unqualified for their current jobs. I was very grateful for the person who raised their hand and asked for clarification. That would have been a terrible message to leave with the group. Encourage and reward honesty, and be sure you are honest in return. It generates and reinforces trust.

Encourage and reward honesty

Include Your Staff Members in the Solution Process

Sometimes your department may be under fire, and you need to make some changes. What do you do? I once had a situation in which I had been told our customer felt the QA department was lazy. After significant investigation, it turned out they thought we were lazy because we allowed food in the lab, and they felt that people who were eating weren't working. On the contrary, by allowing food in the lab, people worked through breaks and lunchtime, and we were able to get maximum utilization of the equipment. The customer would not be convinced that this was an efficient way to work. They felt that chip bags and Coke cans in the lab indicated slovenly test habits. Rather than make a no food ruling that would be seen as a significant negative to the work environment, I called a meeting with the entire department. We discussed the problem and reached the agreement that all food and drink would vanish from the lab when the customer was on the premises. At all other times, food was acceptable. Since they had been included in the problem resolution and had agreed to the solution, the group complied with the new rules and even enjoyed being part of the conspiracy.

If your problem is such that you can include your team into the solution process, do so. It allows them to see some of the issues you are dealing with, and makes them a part of the overall organization. In addition to getting your group comfortable with you, it's also a good idea to make friends elsewhere in the organization. Create a solid, open working relationship with your peers; particularly the development peers. They can be your strongest allies or your worst enemies. You choose. You will almost always win your battle for more resources if you can present your case with backup from the development manager. You will almost always lose the battle if you don't have that backing. It is up to you to cultivate these valuable friendships and alliances. It may cost you a few lunches, but hey. You were going to eat anyway.

8 Leading the Perfect Beast

How to Be an Effective Manager

In this section, we'll talk about how to be an effective manager. This will include tips on self-awareness regarding your role now that your business life is exposed and under the microscope. We'll also discuss how to project yourself inside and outside your department, and how to manage those interactions effectively. Being an effective manager means your people and the people with whom you interact can communicate with you effectively. We'll look at the uses and misuses of meetings, and the wonders of status reports.

Would I want to work for me?

What is the most important characteristic of a good manager? I think it is honesty. As a manager, you have to be honest with your people and with yourself. You have weaknesses. You are going to make mistakes, so be prepared to recognize these errors in judgment, and be ready to admit them. People will respect you for admitting it when you have been in error. It will send a signal that you will allow them to make mistakes too, and they will be more apt to admit it when it happens. Honesty saves a lot of time and effort, and an honest answer is much easier to remember than a fictitious one.

And, what is the other most important characteristic of a good manager? No, it's not good hair, although that always helps. It is consistency. If you are consistent, you are predictable. People will be comfortable dealing with you if you're predictable. Have you ever worked for or with someone who is unpredictable? I have. It drove me crazy. After awhile you just want to avoid that person because you never know how they'll react.

If you're being consistent and honest with your people, they will trust you. Trust will keep your group together through the good and bad times. If you have been honest with your people and they know you're looking out for them, you'll be able to deliver bad news without destroying your department. People will be in it with you for the long run. How can you verify if you are meeting your management goals? Ask yourself, "Would I

If you're consistent and honest with your people, they will trust you and be comfortable with you

want to work for me?" If you can answer that question with a resounding "yes," you're doing things right. Don't forget to ask yourself that question about once a month. It will keep you thinking about being consistent, honest, and fair.

Life under the Microscope

You have moved into the petri dish of management. Now you need to be prepared to have your every statement and motion examined for hidden meaning. This is particularly true when you are new to the position or when you have new people. It will also occur if the company is having problems and people are worried about their jobs. One easy solution to this problem is to keep people so busy with their own work that they don't have time to worry about what you're doing. That may not be possible though. The only way to squiggle out from under the microscope is to make everyone comfortable by creating an honest and open environment. But be aware, it is inevitable that there will always be a few who will be watching your every move.

I always have to be very careful of comments I may make, particularly ones that could be taken out of context. Also, watch the non-verbal communication. If you're walking around with your arms crossed all the time, you might want to mention that you're doing it because you're taking a break from your arctic office, not because you are annoyed. Everyone brings some amount of baggage to work, and you may unwittingly display a characteristic that may have meant something when a previous boss did it. I came into one department whose previous manager had always made rounds at 5:00 pm to see who was still working. I was innocently wandering around one day at that time and couldn't understand why my normally friendly group was suddenly very formal. It wasn't until the next day when someone told me about the previous boss that I understood. I made sure not to wander at that time anymore.

Friends at Work

You really need to get a dog! If you have friends who work for you, you have special considerations. There is always a certain amount of jealousy in any department, and the more popular you are as a manager, the more jealous people will be of those who are close to you. You must be extremely vigilant when talking work with friends, particularly friends whom you trust. You can't confide information to your friends that you wouldn't confide to other individuals in the department in the same position. This can be very difficult to do, particularly if you are in a tough situation and could use some advice. Time to get that dog again!

Even if you don't confide in your friends, there will be an assumption that you do. There's nothing you can do about this except to let time prove that you really don't confide in them. Eventually, it will become apparent that your friend doesn't know any more than their co-workers and the rumors will subside. But, what about going to lunch? That's your time to do what you want with whom you want, right? Right. But again, the assumptions will be that you're doing some confiding, so be careful. Try to spread around your lunches, and invite other people along. Once they know it is not a private club used to discuss the innermost secrets of the department, your eating habits will become less interesting.

But, I'm Hungry!

On the flip side, what about inviting yourself along with a group? There are two sides to that equation. Often, your group won't invite you along because they think you wouldn't want to go with them. In that case, asking if you can come along can be a very positive move. They'll be flattered that you want to go with them. On the other hand, for a variety of reasons, your group may want to go out to lunch without you. I had a boss whom I liked on a personal level, but having lunch with him always resulted in long discussions about work and schedules. That's not how I want to spend my lunchtime. I've also worked for people from whom I needed to get away for a while. The last thing I wanted to do was have lunch with them. So be sensitive to these issues. If you see a group going to lunch and you'd like to join them, ask where they are going. If they hesitate, back off. If they invite you along, you're probably welcome. Once you're out with them, don't try to control the conversation. Just be a part of the group.

If you have managers or leads working for you, watch to make sure they don't make these socializing mistakes. It's a particularly easy error for a new lead to make when they've been promoted from within and already have a set of friends. They should keep their friends, but also remember to keep confidences as well. The newly promoted lead is likely to be pumped for information which can be very hard to resist, particularly if they have juicy information that they could impart. Also, keep an eye out for partiality.

It is so easy for a new manager or lead to give the more interesting work to the people they like. Your job as their manager is to be sure the work is allocated fairly based on ability and availability.

You don't have to like the people who work for you.

One important thing to remember: You don't have to like the people who work for you. It is easier and more fun if you do, but it's likely that you will always have someone you don't like or with whom you aren't comfortable. Regardless, you must treat your employees equally, and judge them on their job performance only. There's nothing you can do about your likes and dislikes – you're human too – but you do need to be aware of why you don't like the person, and sort out what is a personal issue versus what should affect your professional relationship.

Effective Leadership – Looking Outward

Like it or not, you are now a window into your department. Depending on how your department is structured, you may be THE window into your department. You need to have consistent policies and procedures, and you need to represent these. For example, if you have a policy that you won't accept a release without summary release notes, don't be the one who breaks the rules and accepts the undocumented release. Would you be happy if one of your people did that? When I was in college, I worked for Sears in the customer service department. There were many rules about accepting returns, refund policies, check acceptance, etc. As a dedicated employee, I did my best to make these rules clear to the customer. Unfortunately for me, if a customer didn't like the rules and requested to talk to a store manager, the store manager would almost always override them. This made the sneering customer happy, but it sure made me feel foolish. The lesson here is, don't break your own rules. You need to be clear about what you represent. If you have been sending a strong message about QA presence in all design meetings, don't be the one who doesn't show up for the meeting.

It is also very important that you are clear about what you expect from other departments. Here, your well-designed test plan that lays out the rules of engagement becomes a critical tool. You need to establish key relationships and get agreement on the processes that will be used. Be sure to identify the key players in other departments and establish the appropriate contacts within your department to facilitate efficient communication.

Determine how often you will attend project meetings. Do you need to be there to show support for your project leader? Will they think you're checking up on them? Is there an expectation that you will go to those meetings on a regular basis?

There will probably be a few high exposure mistakes that will point back to your department. How will you handle those? I worked for a company where we had to do some of our testing against the engineering mail server. Once in awhile, our testing crashed the machine because we had forgotten to isolate our environment. Oops! We established the policy of declaring a "Klondike." This meant that whoever caused the problem that inconvenienced others, had to go to the local store and buy Klondike bars for everyone. By the time the culprit returned with the treat, the server was back up and all was forgiven. I'm still wondering if some of those outages were intentional! Mistakes will happen. Be ready to accept responsibility, make the appropriate apologies, and provide the correct bribery. But, learn from your errors. You should only do stress testing on the corporate backbone once!

Declare a "Klondike"

Effective Leadership – Looking Inward

As a manager, and particularly if you are a new manager, it is critical that you share your expectations for your department. It is equally critical that people understand the external expectations for the department. Be sure to clearly articulate your expectations and how they are affected by the company goals. For example, I had a department in which I was doing a major reorganization. I wanted the team members to embrace the newcomers and provide the necessary training to get them up to speed as quickly as possible. I asked them to do this because of the company's expectation for my department. The executives planned to use the quality of my department as a key factor in procuring future development business. This was a big goal - and we were a big part of it. As I explained my expectations for the training and assimilation of new employees, I also explained how this was part of the overall scheme to improve our reputation and create a world class testing organization. Once people knew why we were making personnel changes, they were more willing to work with the new folks and were happy to learn they had been selected to become the basis for the new team.

What do you do if the expectations for your department are not realistic? Unfortunately, this happens. It is very important not to let your group become demoralized about goals which they can't possibly attain. While you fight the battle with your management to make realistic and achievable goals, you need to get your team aligned to move toward the goals you expect to meet. Don't complain to them that you have been given unrealistic goals. That's your problem to solve, not theirs to worry about. This is why you make the big bucks!

Now we know why we make the big bucks!

It is important for your team to understand the overall company goals, and the long-term department goals. This helps them know there is a plan and there is a future. Keeping them aware of this information gives them an opportunity to bring forward ideas that may help. If you make them aware of the challenge, they can back you up and articulate the long-term goals if asked. If you work for someone who is likely to stop people in the halls and quiz them on the long-term plans, it behooves you to make your people knowledgeable about what those plans are.

If your long-term plans will require changes to the current personnel or procedures, be sure to allow enough time to establish a comfort level with the proposed changes. It is easier if people understand the reasons for the changes. They may not agree, but at least they will have the background information. Always explain the reasons for changes to established procedures. There are probably reasons for the way things are currently done. If a procedure seems stupid, don't assume it is; assume you don't understand. Before you make changes, ask for input and listen to what you are told; you might learn something!

Effective Leadership – Handling Information

A major part of being an effective leader is handling information. You have to establish a way for information to flow down from you and up to you. Without information, your department will be starved and will make ill-informed decisions. Without information, you will be working on partial data and assumptions, and you will quickly lose the respect of those who work for you.

One part of handling information is keeping track of it. As a manager, you will be stopped in the hallway six times on your way to the lab to look at a problem. Will you remember all six of those interruptions? Will you remember why you were going to the lab? Handling information is a matter of being organized. There are a number of organization seminars available (mostly pushing their products), if you are interested in learning new techniques. You know where you need to make improvements. The point here is that whatever system you use, make sure you don't forget things. If one of your people stops you in the lab and says, "I have to take tomorrow off because I have to take my son to the doctor," you need to remember that fact so you aren't searching for the guy the next day.

How do you remember things? For me, I have to write them down. I'll write them on whatever I have handy (yes, even my hand if that's the only thing around), and then copy them to my complex task tracking system (that's right, yellow sticky notes) when I get back to my office. If I don't write something down, I'm likely to forget it after 20 more interruptions have been put on my stack. Use whatever system and method works for you. Just don't forget an item. If you forget someone's vacation request, they'll take it personally. If you forget to order some item of equipment that had been requested, the person making the request may assume you don't really want them to work on that project. They may not remind you about it, having taken your lack of action as disapproval.

There's nothing wrong with using yellow sticky notes to keep yourself organized … unless your office is windy

Because I have been known to lose track of items that weren't written down, I usually talk to the person about their request, give them my approval, and then ask them to send me an email so I don't forget. Now they understand that I know I sometimes forget things. They'll be more forgiving in the future.

Now where were we … Oh, I remember.

Meetings, Meetings, and More Meetings – Zzzzzzzzz!

As a manager or lead, you will spend a significant amount of your time in meetings. I'm sorry, but it's true. These will be meetings you attend, and meetings you conduct. There are a few simple rules to follow that have worked for me to make meetings more useful and less disruptive to the general flow of work. Most effective meetings last less than one hour. People don't have a very long attention span. An hour is about the maximum effective time for most meetings. You will also find it easier to get people to attend a meeting when it is scheduled for a short duration. Effective meetings require a clear agenda that is understood by the leader and the attendees. If people need time to prepare for a meeting, you need to tell them what it will be about. Meetings are more prompt and much more efficient if the attendees are ready to talk about the subject at hand. I once worked for a VP who would show up to a meeting with no notes, sit down, and say, "So, what's this meeting about?" We learned quickly not to expect any learned input from him!

Keep meetings to an hour or less

It is a matter of courtesy and practicality to respect the time of your attendees. If they are sitting in your meeting, they're not doing anything else. Is your meeting that important? When you are planning your meeting attendees, be sure you are inviting the proper people. Do you really need the VP of Engineering in your schedule meeting, or will a development manager do just as well? Be sure the people you are inviting are the people who can and will actively participate. Don't invite a bunch of VPs just so your meeting appears to be more important.

I believe meetings would be much more carefully planned, and attendees selected with more discretion if there was a time clock on the outside of all conference rooms. Think about it. If each meeting attendee clocked in at the beginning of the meeting and out at the end, and the meeting owner's department was charged for the salaries that sat in at that meeting, it would likely cause some serious reconsideration to the frequency, effectiveness, and attendance of meetings. So, the next time you call a meeting, be sure you know what you want to accomplish and have an efficient plan to do so. I once had a department of about 40 people. That meant if I had a one-hour meeting and required everyone to be there, it cost me one man-week. After doing some objective thinking, I discovered that I rarely needed to have the entire group in a single meeting. People were working on different, non-overlapping projects. It was unusual if I had something to communicate that affected the entire group.

On the other hand, I have been criticized by less open-minded management for not having regularly scheduled weekly staff meetings. Because that was the communication means they favored, they felt that should be applied at all levels. In most cases I got around having the grand meetings by having regularly scheduled project meetings. And, in one case, I instituted a monthly group lunch so we could have our "scheduled" meeting then.

Who Should You Meet With, and When?

As with the above department meeting rules, you meet with the affected group when you have information to impart. Don't include people who are not affected just because you like an audience. And, you shouldn't have the meeting just because it's Tuesday and you always have a meeting on Tuesday at 1:00. Have the meeting because you need to have it. This seems obvious, but look around your company. How many meetings are held only because of tradition?

Having said this, it is only fair to admit there is one big advantage to regularly scheduled meetings, particularly at the project level. People will block out this time on their calendars and they will be available. You don't have to round them up each time you want to have a meeting. Also, this may save you some interruptions if people will hold off on non-critical discussion items until the meeting, rather than disrupting other work.

We're Going to Do WHAT?

There are times when you should meet with just your project leads or managers. This usually happens when you have high-level project specific meetings that overlap areas. Major schedule and resource adjustment meetings will also require the input from your cross-project leaders. Sometimes you need to get your leaders together to pre-announce something you will soon be telling the entire department. It's extremely important to get your people with you before you make an announcement that will cause some level of discomfort in the department. Be sure you give your leaders adequate information to deal with the questions that will undoubtedly be asked. It is dangerous to assume that the important questions will come up in the general announcement meeting, and you should not assume that the important questions will ever get to you.

In some cases (particularly for an announcement regarding company business), you may be able to give your leads and managers more information than you could impart to all levels within your organization. For example, if there has been a pre-announcement that the sales figures are in big trouble for the quarter, you may be able to share exact numbers with your leads and managers, but that information may be too confidential to share at the lower levels. By sharing this type of information, you bring your leads and managers into your circle of confidence, emphasizing that their new role is different than before and they're entitled to confidential information. This helps build their maturity and their trust in you because you have exhibited trust in them.

Be sure your message is appropriate for your audience

Everyone Needs to Know This!

If you decide that you have information that's appropriate for an "all hands" meeting, plan your time wisely. You should prepare a formal presentation, just as you would for your management. This makes your people feel like you have taken the time to prepare, and it helps them to take the information seriously. Be sure to use "all hands" meetings for good news as well as bad. You don't want everyone to cringe when you announce a meeting. When you have concluded what you planned to say, prompt for questions. In some cases, particularly with a shy or large group, it may be hard to get them to ask questions. If you know this is a problem with your group, you might want to do some seeding. Use your leads to ask a few questions and get the conversation going.

When you are determining how you will communicate, you have to consider how you are most effective. I prefer the Management By Walking Around (MBWA) method to having formal meetings. I still have regular project meetings, but only for specific subjects. For general information and for keeping my finger on the pulse of what's happening in my department, I do much better by wandering. You do have to be careful that you don't favor the people who are working on projects that are most interesting to you. It's difficult to be sure you touch everyone equally without actually playing duck, duck, goose. Again, if you have a lab, hang out in it. That's where people are and that's where the work gets done.

One-to-One

The one-to-one meeting is a popular phenomenon in some companies. Theoretically, this gives your people a chance to communicate with you when they have your undivided attention. A one-to-one meeting can be an effective tool for opening communication. One-to-one meetings can also have people cowering in terror when it's their turn. You have to decide what works best in your work environment.

If you decide that one-to-ones are a good plan for you, be sure to set up the schedule for the meetings and allocate enough time. One-to-ones must be held with all your people who are at the same level. If you do one-to-ones with project leads, you need to do them with all the project leads and at the same intervals. And, don't rely on this meeting as your only communication method. It can be very easy to assume that since you have regularly scheduled meetings with people, you know what is going on with them. The one-to-one may not be effective for each person – some people might be intimidated by having to sit across your desk and actually talk to you.

Are there other ways to effectively disseminate information? Sure. How about sending a weekly email after staff meetings with your manager? Email is an effective means of communication, and it keeps everyone informed without imposing on their time. And don't forget the grapevine. If you want information to get out fast, this all-powerful, informal communication path may be your best means. Use both casual and formal environments to communicate based on the message you're sending and the audience. The most important point is that you both impart and gather. Your people have information you will want to receive. Be sure you provide a forum. That doesn't mean you announce your open door policy and then hide behind your desk waiting for people to present you with information. It won't happen. Or, if it does, the information will be out of date. You have to be a part of your group and that includes being part of the information network.

Getting Information – Status Reports

I have found that one of the best sources of information on individuals and projects is a regular status report. A good status reporting system provides each person with a clear channel to you. Weekly reports also give you a great basis for evaluating performance. People have no grounds to complain that you don't know what they do; if they're doing tasks that aren't in their status report – whose fault is that? Status reports also give you an opportunity to provide prompt feedback to the individual.

Ten minutes should be enough time spent on a weekly status report

In most environments, status reports should be done on a weekly basis. Longer durations than that tend to lose the details. Status reports should include four main items:

- What did you do?
- What are you working on now?
- What are you planning to do next week?
- Are there any problems or issues?

Be sure to keep the format simple, and the reports short. It shouldn't take anyone longer than ten minutes to do their weekly status report. Require that the reports be turned in by close of business (COB) at the end of the week. If you let the report wait until after the weekend, it's hard to remember what was done the previous week. Always read every word of every status report. This seems obvious, but I've worked for managers who obviously didn't read my status report (I know this because I put "Mary had a little lamb" in the middle of one… I'm a bad employee). Promptly answer any questions or issues. Not only does this prove you've read the reports, it also proves you're interested in what they say. Remember, if you don't have time to read the reports, why did you ask for them? Should your people be spending time generating paperwork that you won't read? Be sure the status reports are required. Ask where they are if you don't get them. By reminding people that you want their reports, you're also reminding them that you're interested in what they're doing. Unless you are a wholly evil boss (and you better not be after reading this book), your people want you to be interested in their work.

When I started out requiring status reports, I did it primarily because I wanted the data. I found a few side benefits too. By writing a weekly status report, people had to think about what they had actually accomplished compared to what they planned to accomplish. This helped them to stay on track by making quick self-corrections. When I reviewed the reports, I would compare the current week to the previous week, and see if adequate progress was being made. This made it easy for me to spot trouble areas, and block problems that I needed to deal with. Without this early warning system, I probably wouldn't have been aware of some of the minor issues until they became major ones. You will also find that the status report allows you to make timely redirections before too much effort has been expended in the wrong direction or on the wrong project.

By reading the weekly status reports from your group, you can keep yourself well informed about what each individual is doing. You can also watch for frustration areas and issues that are starting to arise. If you have a large department, you may want individual status reports to be turned in to the project leads, then compiled and sent to you. You get less reading that way, but also less information. Personally, I like to get a formal summary from my leads on the projects, but I still like to read the details on the individual status reports.

People may gripe about having to write status reports, but despite all the grumbling, people usually keep copies of their status reports and refer back to them for specific date and event information. They will also use them as input for their annual reviews, and ammunition when they seek a promotion. A good status report has all significant contributions documented. It's a detailed record of someone's career, broken into weekly increments.

9 Evaluating the Perfect (or Maybe Not-So-Perfect) Beast

In this section, we will discuss writing and conducting formal performance evaluations, as well as presenting a merit increase. First, a few words on informal evaluations. Your success as a manager will be largely determined by your ability to effectively use informal feedback. This is your tool to fix problems early, meanwhile encouraging and rewarding the behavior you want to see. In order for it to be effective, informal feedback must be warranted. I once worked for a manager who started each of our one-to-one meetings with, "You're doing a great job." Based on what? Did he even know what I did? These words quickly became meaningless because he didn't associate his words with any particular actions on my part. If he had said, "You did a great job on this test plan. I just read it and have a few comments …" I would have taken his words as sincere and interested.

Be sure that your informal feedback doesn't appear scheduled. I worked with a manager who had a policy of calling the individuals in her group on Monday morning before working hours and leaving each of them a voicemail telling them they were doing a good job. This quickly became a joke within the group as they listened to their weekly pat-on-the-head message.

Informal Feedback

It can be difficult to remember to give positive informal feedback. As a manager, you have to watch for occasions that warrant positive feedback, and act quickly to offer it. I once had an employee who was very talented but very lazy, and sometimes made noticeable mistakes. On the other hand, he periodically did something brilliant. Each time he was clever, I made sure to send him an email so he would have documented proof that I appreciated his good work. He printed out each "atta-boy," as he called them, and pinned them to the wall of his cubicle. Subsequently, any time I approached him with a mistake he had made, he'd quickly hand me one of the atta-boys and declare us even. Funny guy. But, it did help to balance out my annoyance with his errors when I remembered his flashes of brilliance.

This example brings out an important point. Take the time to document your praise. It is great to stop someone in the hall and compliment them on a particular piece of work, but it is more meaningful to them if you write a quick email to confirm your words. A complimentary email will be remembered longer. If the person works for another department, be sure to copy their manager also.

Formal Reviews

Formal reviews are checkpoints for progress toward long-term goals

Formal performance reviews are standard, expected documents. A performance review is not a management tool, but rather a formal written document noting all the performance aspects of the job as you have discussed them with the employee throughout the year. What? You didn't already discuss with them everything that is on the review? Then you haven't been doing your job. The review should just be a formalization of what is already understood between you and your employee.

When thinking in terms of the formal review, it helps to assume that the employee/manager relationship is long-term. This is your checkpoint that your long-term goals for the employee and their long-term career goals are in sync and you are both happy with the progress. Any short-term goals should have been addressed in informal feedback sessions and the weekly status report feedback.

How often should formal reviews be done? Personally, I prefer the annual review because this is not a major coaching tool. Six-month reviews are acceptable, but they can create a lot of overhead in a large department. If quarterly reviews are used, there is a tendency to put off discussions until review time. That's too long to wait if there is a problem. It is easy to procrastinate, particularly if the conversation will be a difficult one – you don't need more excuses. I have seen the more frequent formal reviews become a crutch for people who are ineffective at providing informal feedback.

Getting Your Data Together

No matter what the frequency of the reviews, do them on time. There is no excuse for a late review. If your person can manage to show up for work each day, you can certainly find the time to do their annual review on schedule. You owe it to them. Start planning now. I take at least eight hours to write a review, sometimes longer. That takes planning if you have to do all the reviews at the end of the year, and still get your Christmas shopping done.

There is no excuse for a late review

Reviews should be a mutual evaluation process; the employee should actively participate. Ask the employee to identify their five most important accomplishments during the review period. They should be able to supply a paragraph or two on each of these accomplishments, and explain why it was important to the company. If they don't understand why they do what they do, you need to be doing some clarification. The more details they can give you on their accomplishments, the better. This shows they understood what they did, and it allows them to present to you their finest work. Their input also gives you a basis for discussing what they think is important, which may or may not coincide what you think is important.

"I Didn't Think That Was Important"

I have frequently had people list five major accomplishments and leave out two that were really important. When I asked them why they left those out, they explained that they didn't think those things mattered that much. Now, that may have been my fault. I didn't give them the positive feedback on how important their contribution was to the overall game. I had a guy who worked for me who set up a supposedly impossible network configuration (per the vendor), that was desperately needed for a sales demonstration. He spent a few days on the task, and got it working in time for the demonstration. We got the sale, and he was told at the time that his contribution played a significant role. When I received his review input, he hadn't mentioned this item. When I asked him about it, he said, "Well, I only spent a couple of days on it and it wasn't that much work." That may be true, but it was a high exposure accomplishment, and I wanted it on his review to support my case when I went to my manager to request a bonus for him.

Once you get the employee's input, compare it with what you think they accomplished. Now is the time for you to review their status reports to refresh your memory about the entire year. If you find accomplishments they've missed, be sure to add them to the review document. They will be flattered that you remembered these things, and will know you're looking out for them. Carefully evaluate your opinion of their accomplishments. Now put the review away for a few days and think about it.

Make Time

Watch for those haloes and horns

You need to devote serious time to writing a review. If you can't get the uninterrupted time at work, plan to take it home or work on it during your off hours. Writing reviews takes concentration. You have to evaluate and recall the person's performance over the course of an entire year. Be sure to refer to your notes as you write the review and weigh each event appropriately for its relative importance. Watch the halo and the horn effects. The halo effect is when someone has just done something glorious and you are happy with them, though that one recent thing may not be representative of their performance throughout the year. Conversely, the horn effect occurs when someone has just done something hideous, and that is in the forefront of your mind. I had one of my most reliable, conscientious people accidentally wipe out our main test system (for you UNIX folks, rm –r *.* in the root directory). We had backups, but had to suffer through our own buggy restore program. It was a mistake that anyone could have made, but unfortunately, she did it while I was in the process of working on her review. That was one I had to put aside for a week until I could objectively evaluate her performance again.

When working on a review, take your time. Your employee gave you a year of effort and work; you can certainly spend a day or two on their review. Don't do several reviews in a single sitting, or they will all sound alike. This is particularly difficult when you are doing all annual evaluations at the same time for a large department. When faced with that scenario, it is a good idea to start the reviews a month in advance so you have adequate time to devote to each person.

Using Evaluation Categories

While writing the review, be sure you are using evaluation categories that make sense for the job. Most companies have a standard form, but the categories may not suit the job your department is doing. If this is the case, follow the form, but add your own categories that make sense. I have found the following categories give comprehensive coverage for almost any technical job.

- Planning/Scheduling
- Recommending/Evaluating/Designing
- Interpersonal Relations
- Communication
- Job Knowledge
- Quality
- Productivity

For each of these categories, use specific examples of how well the person has performed their tasks within the context of the category. For example, has this person been productive? Has their work output been acceptable? Have they facilitated other people in getting their jobs done?

Be sure to read the previous review for this person, then put it away. Follow up on any "needs improvement" areas, but don't be repetitive. Sometimes it works well to write the new review, and then check the old one to see if you missed any points you need to cover.

Be Constructive

One of the most important rules is to be constructive. Be sure you are commenting on items that affect job performance, which the person has the power to change. This is not the time to comment on someone's personal crises unless they have affected their job performance. If you have a chronically depressed person working for you, but it's not affecting job performance in any way, this isn't the place to make a note of it. If there is a negative issue and it is affecting job performance, you should have already discussed it; it should be formally documented on the written review. All the while, it is very important to keep your comments professional. For some reason, I'll never understand why people are very prone to share their review with others if it is a negative one. This makes it even more critical to be sure your comments are completely objective, and backed up with specific examples of unacceptable behavior.

Each person is different, and the way they receive a review will vary. It helps to know your person well enough to predict how the information will be taken. If you have someone who will go over the review in

Anticipate how the review will be received

excruciating detail, questioning every word you use, it will pay to have another manager read the review before you present it. I once put the following sentence in a review: "This year Fred has done an excellent job preparing release documentation." When I had another manager review it, he asked if I meant to imply that in previous years Fred had done a less than excellent job. Since that certainly wasn't what I meant, I changed the wording.

Conducting the Review

Listen carefully   Each employee deserves your undivided attention when review time comes. Set aside the time, and be sure you will not be interrupted. Since you will now be writing thorough and detailed reviews, you may want to consider letting the person read the review prior to meeting with them. This gives them a chance to absorb the information you're conveying, and lets them evaluate and react to what you've said. Then, when you meet, they've had time to get their thoughts in order and are ready to discuss what you've written.

When you're conducting the review, in addition to going over what you've written, you may also want to bring up any items you'd like to discuss (but didn't warrant being formally recorded on the review). If you work for a manager who tends to overreact, you may want to be very careful about what you put on the written review; you wouldn't want to escalate a minor issue. Your manager may be more intolerant of areas needing improvement than you are, so it may be wise to address these items verbally.

As you conduct the review, walk through the written document and discuss each major section. Allow adequate opportunity for questions and discussions. Be sure to listen and clarify as needed. This is the time the employee is likely to bring up things that have been bothering them, and things they would like to see changed. It is also a good opportunity to discuss career goals, making sure your plans align with the employee's goals. This is not the time to pacify – it's the time to be honest.

If a merit increase is tied to the review, deliver the raise at the conclusion of the discussion of the review. Some companies believe in separating this process. You will have to follow the rules that are dictated in this area. Generally, you've been given a budget to work with and you have some discretion in determining the amount of the raise. We'll discuss some methods for determining salary increases in the next section. Tell your employee as much as you can about the raise process, how their raise was determined, and where it falls relative to the rest of the department. The written review should substantiate the performance rating that was the basis for the raise. If it doesn't, you will have a lot of explaining to do!

10 Feeding the Perfect Beast

Effective Reward Systems and Growth Plans

Let's face it: people are working for money. There may be the tiny minority that work for intellectual fulfillment, but the vast majority of us are in it for the money. So, now that we've faced that issue, how are we going to make sure our people get enough of the monetary motivator? In this section we will discuss how to keep the compensation equitable, what makes people stay at a job, and a handy method for figuring out merit increases.

Fodder for the Equity Battle

One of the biggest non-technical problems that confront QA managers in particular is getting adequate, equitable pay for our employees. There is still a stigma associated with quality assurance and the lingering belief that good technical people would aim for development, rather than quality assurance. And, on some days, you might agree that no one with any sense would go into QA as a career! But, we're in the job because we like the challenge, and the equity battle is just another one of the challenges we face.

QA and development must receive equal compensation for equal work

Any experienced QA professional knows that QA compensation must be equivalent to the compensation given to the development staff. This means the salary basis must be the same, as well as the merit increases, bonus pools, and other salary related programs. Position titles can be different (and often will be), but the same position and the same responsibility in either department should receive the same compensation.

OK, we all agree on this. Now, how do we convince our management that equity is a requirement? I've successfully used the following arguments:

Training and Education

Training/experience/education are the same for QA engineers as they are for developers. Note that we're talking about QA engineers here, the technical resources in our department. QA analysts (the non-programming types) are in a different pool, and may have fewer technical requirements, yet more business requirements. In some cases, the QA analyst pay scale is closer to the marketing and business analyst groups. This all depends on how technical your analysts are, what their potential is, and what your expectations are for their performance. For the QA engineers, we are expecting them to be able to program AND to step back and analyze other people's requirements and implementation efforts. They may also be designing and implementing automation systems that are far-reaching in scope and critical to the efficiency and performance of the company. This knowledge and ability is at least equivalent to that expected of the development staff.

Skill Sets and Knowledge

QA work requires unique skill sets and knowledge. It takes time to train a good QA person. Not only do they have to learn the product – as does a developer – and the code (for the white-box folks), as does a developer; they also have to learn the testing methods, automation plans, and documentation requirements of the job. But these are just the technical aspects. It is critical to their success that they also be adept at dealing with all the personalities they encounter in their daily interactions, and that they be able to (dare I say it?) manipulate the interested parties into doing what needs to be done. Now that is a skill you don't just hire off the street! I can take any bright person and teach them to program, write test plans, and document what they do. I can't teach them to be a good people person, or an expert at diplomacy. But, these are invaluable skills that are requirements for an effective QA person.

The company has an internal training investment in your people. Depending on the level of documentation available for your software products, there is undoubtedly a significant amount to be learned and retained. Again, this is an area where the company is likely to have a more significant investment in the QA staff than in the development staff. If there are good programming specs, a new developer can hit the ground running. Regardless of the depth of the specifications and the amount of test documentation, a QA person will only be effective when they've built the requisite relationships that will make them successful.

It is difficult to find and retain good, qualified people. Yet, unfortunately, it can be easy to retain the people you don't want. The best QA people are interested, curious, and always want to be learning. That means you have to provide them with an environment where they can continually improve their skills. Once you've got a system in place where people are comfortable, cross-trained, and learning, be sure you retain them to keep the balance in place. As soon as you're not paying enough money, people will start to migrate to other departments, or worse, to other companies. There is a delicate balance within a happy department where you have the right mix of senior and junior people. Once you get there, you sure don't want to lose anyone for something as silly as inadequate compensation.

Provide an environment that promotes learning

Stay Competitive

Gathering data from other successful companies can help with your battle. There are good companies out there that pay their QA departments well. Find some. Go to conferences and compare salary rates. Interview people and find out what they're making. This will give you data to present to your management, and will help keep your company competitive.

And We Have to Pay Them Too?

Keep in mind that people can't stay at a job if they are not adequately compensated. They may want to stay, but they have to make enough money to meet their needs. While you're trying to make sure your people are happy, be sure you remember to do a periodic reality check. You don't want to be paying people more than they're worth either. At the same time, part of your job is also to ensure that the company is getting its money's worth. It is hard to tell someone they don't deserve a raise, but sometimes it is the honest and right thing to do. If someone has unrealistic expectations about what they should be making, it's up to you to reset those expectations.

One of the biggest challenges to realistic expectations came in the boom of the .com era. People with little experience were landing jobs with whopping salaries. I can still remember having conversations with individuals who would come to my office and say, "I have a friend who has less experience than me and he just got a job at Aren'tWeCool.com for a bazillion dollars. I want a raise." Faced with this, I'd go through the advantages of staying with our company, which was stable and public, and would still be in business next year. For some of the more adventurous types, they chose to try the startup world. I gave them my honest advice and wished them well in their pursuits. Some were very happy that they changed; most came back again.

Higher paying jobs are probably out there

Remember that most people can get a higher paying job if they try – therefore it is vital to be sure that working for you is providing them with a balance that gives overall job satisfaction. They must perceive that they are receiving adequate compensation. They also have to be satisfied with their job most of the time. No one likes their job all the time; there are always negative things about a job. Your goal should be to provide a work environment where job satisfaction is there for the taking. It's a worthwhile exercise to write down what you think gives your employees job satisfaction. Have a staff meeting, and compare your answers with theirs. And, while you're at it, figure out what gives you job satisfaction too. This will help you to build your own career.

Your manager might not be as good a manager as you are (or will be after you finish this book), so you might want to share your job satisfaction criteria with him under the pretense of discussing job satisfaction for your group. That approach is less confrontational and allows you to open the conversation without putting him on the defensive. Remember, as Cem Kaner notes in his book *Testing Computer Software* (Wiley, 1999, p. 344), there is an extremely high turnover in test managers. Why is that? Job satisfaction can be difficult to attain. You must work at it.

Stop That Resume!

Most people don't want to do the work of updating their resume. If they do put in that effort, it's really easy to post it to the web, and if the job market is good and they are qualified, they're very likely to pick up a new job. The trick is to determine what factors make people update their resumes, and be sure you eliminate those factors before the updates occur. I've always thought it would be an excellent indicator of a company's health and likelihood to survive if you could get an honest survey of how many people had a current resume. People who don't keep their resume current aren't likely to be considering changing jobs.

If we work with the assumption that an updated resume will soon lead to an opening in your department, it's worthwhile to think about how to stop those updates. One of the big motivations for changing jobs is the perception that the compensation isn't fair. So what can you do about it? Talk to people and be accessible. If a person wants to talk about improving their situation, they really want to stay. This gives you something to work with, and gives you a chance to protect your training investment.

Be sure your salaries are fair. There's nothing worse than trying to defend your salary structure, and later finding out that your employees are indeed underpaid. Compare your salaries with other companies via surveys, and by asking people you interview. In addition to being sure your people are fairly paid in comparison to other companies, it is also important to be sure there is parity within your group. This has been extremely difficult to maintain in the high tech industry because of the escalating price of new graduates. Your responsibility to your people is to be sure they are paid fairly in comparison to each other. This means that new hires must fit within your existing salary structure according to experience and education levels. That's all fine and good and common sense. Now, what happens when you want to hire someone who doesn't fit within your salary model?

Be sure your salaries are fair

You Make Too Much Money!

First, you need to determine if your offer is adequate for the industry. If so, the prospective employee might be willing to take a cut from their higher paying job in order to join your organization. If not, start lobbying and gathering your data. You must keep your salaries equal to the competition. In this case, the competition is not companies competing with your products, but companies that are competing with you for employees.

If the prospect doesn't fit within your salary model, you want to look for reasons why their current or former company had to pay more. Were they unstable? Were they too new to have an established track record? Also, look at what your company has to offer that might be superior. Do you have a bonus or stock plan? Do you have more interesting technology? Do you have better learning opportunities? When you're looking for arguments to make to your candidate, ask yourself if you would join your company now. If so, why?

You Don't Make Enough Money!

I'm sorry, but I have to pay you more than you requested

On the other hand, what if you want to hire someone whose salary is considerably lower than your pay scale? You need to figure out why it is so low. Was their company having tough financial times and just didn't have the money? Did their skills advance quickly and they were under-promoted in their last job? Are they from a different economic region? I once hired someone from Tennessee for a job in California. He was making about $35,000, and was easily a Senior QA Engineer. My pay scale indicated that he should be making around $60,000 for his experience and education. When I asked him what he expected to make, he said he'd researched it and found that the cost of living in California was considerably higher and felt he should be making about $45,000. I think his research was a bit off. We offered him $60,000, because it was the equitable thing to do. We could have hired him for less money, but that wouldn't have been fair to him, and we would likely have had retention problems. As it was, he was thrilled with the offer and very loyal to the company because he felt we had looked out for his interests.

If you have problems getting people to accept offers, raise the problem with your management and your HR department. Go armed with the facts about the people who turned down offers and the reasons they gave. Losing or not being able to hire the right people can cripple a company in the long run; it's a critical problem that management needs to address.

Rewards – Merit Increases

If you are going to be giving merit increases, you need a plan. Merit increases are usually done from a set pool of money, often a percentage of the overall salary in your department. Even if you will be doling out the increases throughout the year (on anniversary dates for example), you want to do your merit increase planning for the whole department at one time. This can be a rough plan; it may change depending upon an individual's performance throughout the year. Doing the plan for everyone at the same time helps to ensure parity and a consistency in your evaluation criteria.

Use a Rating System

I like to use a rating system when evaluating people. Rather than a number scale, I use a grading scale A-F, much like in school. The rating you give for the merit increase must correspond to the overall rating you gave (or will give) on the performance review. The rating is based on the individual's performance within the specified job. If you are doing your merit planning at the beginning of the year (or more likely at the end of the year for the following year), you are estimating what the performance evaluation will be. If you have had people working for you for several years, this estimate is likely to be very accurate. If you have new people, you'll have to estimate an average performance. The numbers generally balance out.

If I have managers or leads working for me, I have them rate each one of their people using the A-F scale where:

A = Consistently outstanding performance
B = Consistently exceeds expectations
C = Meets the expectations for the job
D = Improvement needed
F = Why haven't I fired this person already?

I also rate each person independently. Then we sit down together and discuss the reasoning behind the ratings. This is an excellent learning opportunity for your leads as they learn how to evaluate people fairly and accurately. It should also be an opportunity for you to learn more about the people working for your leads. You will also have a chance to evaluate how fair and accurate your leads are in their evaluations. If you have significant disagreements, you need to understand where the problems lie. Is a lead failing to see the whole picture? Did they think someone did a great job when you know the person never completed their assignments? Do you have information you didn't pass on to your lead? Is the lead not attentive to the right things? Use this as a training opportunity.

I gave Fred a D.
Why did you give him a B?

I had a manager who consistently rated one of his leads as an A. I rated the lead as a C. Clearly we had a problem. Upon further review, I found that my manager felt the lead was doing an outstanding job because their interaction was very good, and the work got done on time and correctly. Unfortunately, what the manager wasn't seeing was that the lead's people hated him. He was a tyrant. They worked for him only grudgingly, and while they got the work done, they were all frantically trying to get assigned to different projects. It was a matter of perspective. We compromised and gave him a B rating, and began discussions regarding his problems with people management.

Match Merit to Performance

Merit increases should be awarded based on the expected performance rating. Given that you have five possible ratings, you need to determine how to allocate your merit pool. Since merit increases are usually designated as a percentage of salary, this is where it gets tricky. Your highest paid people may be your best performers, but if you give them a high percentage merit increase, you may use up your entire budget. But, you can play with the numbers after completing your evaluations. First, take the amount you have budgeted and divide it across the ratings. If you have a pool of 5% of your salaries, you might want to allocate it the following way:

A = 8%
B = 6%
C = 4%
D = 2%

Even though your pool is 5% and you might think your average raise for your C performer should be 5%, that would limit your ability to significantly reward your higher performers. You want to keep your A's and B's happy, even if it costs some grumbling from your C's. And if your D's get mad and quit, so much the better. As you can see, when you're playing with these numbers, this is the one time you value your low performers! They help free up money you can give to your top performers.

What do you do if your raise pool is abysmally small (other than sulk)? Tell your people as soon as you can. If you're allowed to, tell them the pool amount and tell them why the amount is so low. People will accept a smaller raise if they know everyone is getting a smaller raise due to lower than expected company sales. Some people may be unhappy enough to leave, but they would undoubtedly have left when they got their itty-bitty raise anyway. It's healthier for a group to get the bad news at the same time and grumble together than to think they're being mistreated individually. It is a lot easier to give the little raises throughout the year if everyone already has their expectations set low. If your company is not giving merit increases due to economic reasons, be sure you let people know. This is one of those times to have the big group meeting. Be honest about the situation and explain what you know. People won't like the news, but it's better to set the expectation.

What do you do if the raise pool is very large (other than celebrate)? Be sure to explain to your people why the pool is big, and set the expectations that subsequent years are likely to be smaller. You don't want to set an expectation that raises will always be 10% or higher! On the other hand, if merit raises are always 10% or higher, send me the name of your company…

Rewards – Seeking Alternatives

Merit raises aren't the only means of rewarding employees. Look around for good ideas for creating other reward systems. What are other parts of the organization doing? Do they have any ideas you could mimic? Consider creating a reward system that works for the whole project team. People in different departments will compare notes, so be sure rewards given between departments are equitable. You don't want to be giving $5 McDonald's gift certificates while another department on the same project is getting a free trip to Disney World.

Type of Rewards

One of the most successful reward programs I've heard of (and been involved in) has been the "night-on-the-town" award. This is a small monetary award from $150-$300, which compensates the employee and a date. It's a great way to pay back long hours on a short project. It's also a good way to recognize the sacrifice of the employee's spouse or significant other. This is a particularly effective reward if a person can be nominated for it by anyone in the company – a co-worker, another manager, or someone from another department. It does a lot for department morale when a developer nominates a tester in recognition of their contribution to a project.

There are many types of recognition awards, which are used to recognize an individual or a team's contribution to a particular effort. Some examples are plaques, statues, T-shirts, certificates, or almost anything that can be displayed. The point of the recognition award is that it be a public declaration of worthiness. Some companies have very creative ideas for the recognition-type awards. Even a silly symbol can be a welcome addition to someone's office if it's presented with the right emphasis and sincerity. Maybe your group gives out the golden flyswatter award for the finder of the biggest bug in a time period. It doesn't have to be an expensive award to be effective.

I heard of one company that had a flying pig award which was given to the person who had the most impossible schedule (as in, the software will ship when pigs fly ...). It wasn't a very politically correct award, but it was good for morale and brought sympathy for the recipient.

If you are designing or revamping an awards system, consider making categories of awards. If you make an award system in which everyone is eligible, everyone will be more interested in participating. Some sample categories are listed below:

- Quality award – Contributions to the quality of a project
- Leadership award – Good leadership at any level
- Lifesaver or Project Saver award – Critical to the success of an important project
- Team Player award – Effective team member who helps other team members be more successful

You can use any categories that work for your organization, just be sure that whatever you chose will be useful over the years. A reward system that dies out quickly becomes counterproductive.

Dealing with Perceived Deservedness

But where's my award?

Perceived deservedness is always an issue with any reward system. Many good reward plans have died under the accusations of "why did he get it and not me?" In order to avoid this sad demise, be sure you make the qualifying parameters for the reward clear. If there is a reason why some people will be excluded, explain it when the system is established. Make it clear if there are frequency rules to the award, and be sure your system is set up so you don't get in the situation where "all the good people already got the award, so who should we vote for now?"

Who will determine the recipients of your awards? If you use popular vote, it's a good idea to require a short paragraph indicating why the person should win. Not only does this let you validate the vote and ensure you're not running a popularity contest, but it also makes the award more meaningful. Reading excerpts from the election notes during the award ceremony will grab everyone's interest and validate the award. If you use management vote to determine the recipients, will there be a grassroots disagreement that this is no longer a recognition award, but just another performance review? Determine *now* if you're going to let management influence the vote in a general election. Sometimes you really do need the veto power. I once had someone nominated for a productivity award. He had indeed been very productive on a particular project. Unfortunately, it was not the project to which he was assigned; it was the one he liked to work on. In truth, his work on the wrong project was actually a performance issue that we had discussed several times. This was not an award I wanted to see him receive.

When you're establishing your program, consider the frequency of the awards and the presentation method. Awards should be given at a scheduled time, such as during quarterly departmental meetings. Annual awards are too infrequent, and people forget who received the reward last and why. If the awards are given more frequently than quarterly, they tend to lose their significance just by sheer volume. Presentation of the awards should be done publicly (well, maybe not the flying pig). Take pictures! Put them in the company newsletter. Make people proud to receive the rewards, and proud to work on projects where awards are given.

Yikes! Bonus Systems!

Bonus systems are very difficult to implement and manage. In many cases, the bonuses cease to be a reward, and become an expectation. When this happens, the bonus is no longer a motivator for extra effort.This can negatively motivate an employee if the amount is reduced, or the bonus is discontinued. Bonuses are indeed a difficult tool to use effectively over a period of several years. Acknowledging this, let's look at the pros and cons of some bonus systems, and some ways to make them work for you.

In general, there are three types of bonuses: scheduled regular bonuses that are considered a part of salary compensation, individual bonuses based on individual or company performance, and project related bonuses.

Compensation Bonuses

Compensation bonuses are those discussed at the time of hire. These are usually based on a percentage of salary, and are often used in companies that don't have stock purchase plans. The purpose of these is to increase employee compensation while keeping base salary rates competitive and palatable to upper management. In these cases, there is usually a published percentage range based on salary or position. The manager determines the actual percentage of the bonus award within the range guidelines. Because expectations are set at hire time, this type of bonus usually has strict rules for administration that must be followed.

This type of bonus is generally not very useful as a motivational tool because there is an expectation that it will be earned by putting forth just an adequate job performance. This can be a huge disincentive if later incarnations of management decide to lower the amount of the bonus, or add new requirements for how the bonus money must be earned. As a manager it is best to keep your people apprised of the rules in place for these bonuses, and be honest as to what their expectations should be.

Individual Performance Bonuses

People need to understand the bonus criteria

Individual, performance-based bonuses are by far the most common, and can be used very effectively as a motivational tool. These bonuses are usually composed of two parts; individual performance goals and company performance goals. Most people's individual contributions can only be vaguely associated with the overall performance of the company, so this part of the bonus is usually considered to be beyond individual control. Concentrate therefore on the individual contribution aspect of the bonus. Some of the most effective systems I've seen use a combination rule. For example, 50% of the amount is determined by the performance of the company, and 50% is determined by the performance of the individual. This combination helps to keep the individual's focus on their own performance as well as an awareness of and a stake in how the company performs.

As with all bonus programs, it is important that the individual understand what they must do to achieve the maximum bonus amount. In order to do this, you must (as a manager) understand how the program is administered, and be able to establish clear goals and the criteria for evaluating how those goals are met. I recommend using a form that requires specifying three to five goals, the evaluation criteria for each goal, and a place to put comments regarding the accomplishment of those goals and a percentage of completion. Say one of your goals is to ship release 2.3 to the field in August. Say you miss your goal and ship it in September instead. If you started on the project in January, a one-month slip could result in a 90% completion of the goal. If the shipment in August was critical to the company's success, perhaps missing the goal by one month could result in a 25% completion or maybe a 0%.

By setting out the evaluation criteria when the goals are established, you save yourself a lot of unhappiness later when the assessment is made. The ideal here is to set bonus criteria that are subjective enough to be useful as a motivational tool, and objective enough that the person can understand the goals and the rules. Try to be as clear and specific as possible while still allowing yourself some latitude for the appraisal.

One other item to remember when setting goals for people is to keep the goals approximately equivalent in required time and effort. That will allow you to do a more equitable distribution of the bonus money based on the evaluation criteria.

Project Bonuses

Project completion bonuses are particularly difficult for QA. They can be very useful as a motivational tool to get a project team to put in a lot of extra effort, but they can have the opposite effect if the project fails to meet the criteria and the reward is not given. It is very difficult to clearly define the rules for a project bonus. This requires careful consideration of the company goals, as well as what is realistically achievable.

When defining the bonus program, it is critical to define what happens if the project deadlines are not met. What if significant effort was made but the final goal wasn't achieved? What if external factors caused the failure? Was the deadline ever possible? Sometimes it is best to use phased deadlines so a percentage of the bonus can be awarded. This can be difficult to sell to a management team that only wants a final result and doesn't care how you get there. It is, however, a more realistic approach to the way work actually gets done. It may be possible to consider a scaled-down bonus depending on effort and achievement of milestones. If your shipment was planned for August, maybe the bonus amount is 110% for

Most project bonuses are based on delivery dates, not quality

shipment in July, 100% for shipment in August, or 75% for shipment in September.

Unfortunately, almost all project bonuses are based on shipment dates, and that puts QA in a bad position. If the project doesn't ship on time, who's likely to be the group holding up the software? That's right, QA. So how do you create a bonus system that produces the desired result – a successful product that ships on time – without putting the QA group in the bad-guy seat?

Make the Bonus Fair for QA

There are several ways to bring the shipment date back into visibility for the entire group. The goal of the bonus system should be to build in quality from the beginning of the project so the whole team is involved in meeting the end goal. If the bonus is paid based on the success of the product in the field after a specified ship date, rather than just meeting the shipment date, suddenly the whole team is concerned that the software actually works when it ships, not just that it ships.

By establishing bonus guidelines that reinforce the importance of the quality of the software, we can help encourage the project team to work toward goals that will benefit the company and the project. Two examples are given below; one showing traditional, quality-unfriendly criteria, and the other showing a sample of criteria that will encourage the team to produce a high-quality product.

Figure 18:
Good and Bad Bonus Criteria

Bad Bonus Criteria

- Project "Cool SW" must ship by February 1st
- Every team member must work at least 60 hours a week
- Only non-management team members are eligible

Good Bonus Criteria

- Project "Cool SW" must complete beta by end of Q1 with fewer than three must-fix problems found in the field in the first three months post-beta
- Team members must facilitate the entire team in meeting its goals

The second example above still provides a goal date, but it requires that the software actually be working at that time. Further, it specifies how the success of the software will be measured; putting the success/failure decision on whether the software works for the customer after it gets there. The ship date doesn't matter. If the team decides to ship earlier and have a longer beta, it can. Most importantly, if the team meets this goal, the company sees a successful product which is delivered on time.

Also specified in these criteria is the caveat that the team members must work together. This gives you (as a manager) the latitude to reduce the bonus for team members who don't work well or assist others on the team. This helps to eliminate the "throw it over the fence" syndrome, where development feels their work is done once the software is handed over to QA. Similarly, it encourages the QA people to get involved early in the project and assist development in getting the software delivered. This is an area that may be difficult to assess, but some subjective latitude is needed in bonus programs.

The example of bad criteria includes a hard shipment date with no indication of what happens if the software ships, but doesn't work. It also requires that people work a specified number of hours a week. While this may ensure that you have a lot of bodies filling chairs, it won't ensure that they are actually getting anything useful done. Requiring people to work long hours may actually reduce productivity (see Tom DeMarco's *The Deadline: A Novel about Project Management* for this exact comment). Another common mistake in the bad criteria example is the exclusion of the management team from the bonus. They need to be just as much a part of the project as the rest of the group. By excluding managers (or even worse, leads), you are creating a caste system; a good team will resent that their manager isn't included in the bonus.

Whatever criteria you decide to use, be sure they are published and well understood by all involved. It is also important that managers in other departments who are not involved in the bonus program be aware that there is one. Other departments will hear that there is a bonus being offered. It is important that their management be able to explain the criteria, and if necessary, explain why their group is excluded from the program.

Evaluating Achievements

When evaluating how well the team performed, there are a number of factors that you may want to consider. This is particularly important if the bonus will be paid out in varying amounts. Some of the areas to consider during the individual evaluation are the following:

- How much did this person contribute to the team's performance in meeting the goal?
- How much effort did this person expend? Remember, you already pay them their salary for working a regular day at a regular pace.
- How was this person's attitude throughout the project? Did they help their co-workers? Were they encouraging and supportive?
- Did this person bring any innovation to the project that made it run more efficiently?
- Did this person supply leadership at any level?

When evaluating individual performance toward the goals set out in the bonus plan, you can use the same A-F rating system you used for the merit increases. I figure if someone gets an F in the rating for a bonus, they actually owe me money! Seriously though, by evaluating the overall team performance to the criteria and the individual's contribution to the team's performance, you can determine a fair and equitable bonus amount for each person.

Unrealistic goals can be discouraging

Bonuses are a quagmire, and you want to wade in with great caution and good leech repellent. Keep your sights on your team's real goals, and establish bonus criteria which will ensure those goals are attained. Be sure the goals you set are realistic; bonus systems with unrealistic goals are at best laughable, and at worst discouraging. Explain the criteria and the evaluation system when the program is created, so everyone will be playing by the same rules. Monitor the progress closely. You want your people to perform the best they possibly can so you can give them the highest reward for their efforts.

Titles and Promotions

Does your title matter to you? Did it matter to you at one time in your career? It's easy to become accustomed to being a manager and carrying a manager-type title. When that happens, it's also easy to forget that once upon a time, you cared a lot if you were called a QA Engineer or a Senior QA Engineer. Just as parents sometimes forget what it was like to be a teenager, we as managers forget what it was like to be starting out and moving up the ranks. Titles and promotions are significant to some employees.

It is important that the QA job titles match the development titles for similar skill sets. If your development group has an Associate Engineer title for folks hired just out of school, QA should have an Associate QA

Engineer title for the same experience level. If your job titles aren't currently structured that way, work with your management, HR, and the development managers to get some standardization in place. This will help you later when you are battling for pay equity. Once you get your job titles established, be sure you use the titles correctly when doing promotions or hiring new folks. Don't break your own rules!

In this section, we're going to discuss establishing promotion criteria, timing the promotions, announcing promotions, and how to handle those who are simply not promotable.

Establishing Promotion Criteria

Promotion criteria should be loose, but clear. You don't want to have job descriptions that will create the expectation of a promotion. For example, if your description for a QA Engineer is 3-5 years of experience, and your Senior QA Engineer description is 5-7 years of experience, you can bet at least half your QA Engineers are expecting a promotion when they complete their fifth year of experience. It would be nice if promotions were so straightforward and automatic, and would require a lot less thought on our part as managers. Reality, though, does exist.

Promotion criteria need to be loose, but clear

I once had a QA Analyst working for me who had about 12 years of experience and wanted to be promoted to Senior QA Analyst. While she was an excellent contributor in many aspects, she was not technically strong enough to hold a senior position. When she asked me when she could expect a promotion, I explained to her that she didn't have the technical expertise required for the position. She said she would learn what she needed to know. Now, in the 12 years she had been working in QA, she never showed an interest in increasing her technical knowledge. Therefore, it seemed a little unlikely to me that she would suddenly become my technical go-to person. We had a long discussion about it, during which I asked her if she was really interested in becoming more technical. Did she want to take classes outside of work? Did she find herself drawn to technical journals? To her credit, she honestly answered that she really wasn't interested in advancing her technical skills; she just wanted the promotion. Then we discussed what benefits she felt she would gain from the promotion. Because our salary structure created large, overlapping ranges of compensation, she would not have made significantly more money as a low end Senior QA Analyst. I also explained to her that if she moved to

But I want a promotion!

that position, she'd be evaluated by different criteria. As a QA Analyst she was getting a consistent B rating, but as a Senior QA Analyst she would be unlikely to get higher than a C-. After this discussion she concluded that she wasn't really suited for the promotion, and the subject didn't come up again. She worked for me for another five years in that same title.

Whom Should I Promote?

When you are defining your promotion guidelines, make it clear that these are only guidelines. Each individual is different, and some are so skilled in some areas that their shortcomings in other areas aren't an issue. When you hire people, be sure you put them in a position that fits your criteria for that job classification. You certainly don't want people to transfer into your department only because they think it is an easy way to get a promotion or a better job title. Your titles and promotion policies need to be consistent with the rest of the organization.

The best organizations and companies I've worked for and with have a dual career path: one for technical, and one for management. You never, never want to force a technical person into a management position simply because it is the only promotion path open to them. This almost always results in a personal, and sometimes a professional, failure. Not only is the person unhappy, so are the people who have to work for them. Be sure your company offers a technical promotion path that goes at least as high as the director path in the management fork. This provides your top technical people with growth opportunities, while giving you an excellent recruiting tool for top technical talent.

Don't promote someone who doesn't want the promotion

I worked with a top-notch technical guy who was a senior developer, and was the architect of most of the company's software. As a "reward" the VP of Engineering promoted him to the position of manager, and gave him responsibility for managing three people. Not only was this done without asking if he wanted the job, he was told about it when it was announced at the engineering department meeting (clearly the company had some other management issues!). He was horrified. He had no interest in a management job whatsoever. Sharing in his horror were the people assigned to him who respected him technically but didn't want to work for him. It was a bad situation for all involved.

Before you decide to promote someone (particularly into a lead or management position), be sure they want it. Just because you chose the management career path, doesn't mean everyone else wants it. Some (like the example above), may view it with true horror (the rest of us figure out the horror part of the job a little later).

Factors to Consider

When you are considering someone for a promotion, you'll want to look at the following factors:

- Education
- Applicable experience
- Job performance at their current level
- Demonstrated responsibility
- Leadership
- Maturity/Attitude

We discussed these characteristics in earlier sections. Take the time to evaluate your candidate carefully, both in their current position and in the one to which you will promote them. The skills that allow them to succeed in their job today may not be the ones they'll need in the new position.

When should you actually promote somebody? Usually at the annual review. In some cases, you may need to do a mid-year promotion, but generally it is better to have people thinking about promotions only once a year. If you want to save yourself some pain and embarrassment, never promise someone a promotion. Their performance may fade over time. They may develop traits that make them unsuitable for promotion. The company policy toward promotions may change. Don't create an expectation you can't fulfill.

When Is My Person Ready to Promote?

Ideally, you'd like to see the person at the top of their game before you actually promote them. Of course, requiring someone to do a job they're not being compensated for really isn't fair. If they chose to do it to demonstrate their ability to take on more responsibility, that's great. If they want to try out the new position and you can give them that opportunity, do it. Just be careful if they want to try out being a lead. Leads, as we've discussed, either have the ability or don't. Your natural leader will already be leading projects before they're promoted. Your "wanna-be" lead won't be leading anything until you give them the authority to do so. In my experience, they don't need your authority if they have the natural ability.

A natural leader will already be leading before the title change

As a safeguard, my general promotion policy is that you have to have at least one year's performance at your current job with an A or B rating. While this isn't a guarantee that the person will continue to perform at that level on the new job, it does show that they are working hard to be one of the better performers.

Announcing promotions requires great diplomacy. I have had a number of engineers working for me who didn't want their promotion to senior engineer announced. Why was that? They felt that their peers already thought of them as senior people, and didn't want everyone to know that they hadn't been. That's OK with me. I adopted the policy that I'd ask each person I promoted if they wanted me to announce it. If so, I'd send out a quick email to the group congratulating the person. If not, I would not make the formal announcement and would instead let the person tell whomever they wanted. If I promote someone to a lead or manager position, I do make the announcement. This is a high-visibility position and I feel it is important that their peers and subordinates know this person has my backing in their new role.

But You're Just Not Promotable

We talked about what to do with someone who isn't promotable. Be honest with them. Explain why they aren't being promoted, and what they'd need to do to close the delta. Offer whatever training and guidance you can, within the scope of the time and money available. Chances are (as in my example above), the person doesn't really want the added responsibility; just the title and/or the money. What if they threaten to leave if they don't get the promotion? Plan a lovely going away lunch. You don't need someone who will be constantly bugging you about a promotion which they don't deserve. Chances are that this is not one of your star performers anyway, or you would be promoting them.

What if the person wants to move into management, but doesn't have the skills for the job? To me, this is one of the most difficult promotion situations. When this has occurred in my departments, the person has had the necessary technical ability and good organization skills, but just isn't good with the people. You hope that they will recognize this shortcoming, but given that they aren't good with people in the first place, they tend to be obtuse about noticing such things. In this case, try to provide whatever training and guidance you can, and then assign them to a technical lead position where they can use their strengths without having personnel responsibilities. While they may object to not being in charge of people, they usually become buried enough with the project tasks that they forget they didn't get all the authority they wanted.

Rewarding Yourself

It took me a long time to figure out why I was no longer getting the job satisfaction I had in the past. I later realized it was because I didn't get the amount of positive feedback I had enjoyed in lower positions. As a leader, you are now responsible for your own job satisfaction. The rewards from a leadership job are quite different from those you received as an individual contributor. You rarely finish a job. You may finish a project, but you have already started the planning on the next one, so you don't even get to breathe a sigh of relief. Your main job now is developing and training your people so that they can get the work done. Growing people is a long-term proposition.

Growing people is a long-term proposition

Rewards Are Now Long-Term

You need to expect your job rewards to be long-term. How can you assess your success in a management job? Ask yourself some of the following questions:

- Do your people stay with you on a job for several years?
- Is your department's turnover rate lower than average for your company?
- Do your leads and managers go on to success in other positions? Is this because you trained them well? Is it because you selected the right people?
- Are you a critical part of the product teams?
- Do people follow you to your next job?
- Is it a loss to the organization when you leave?

Your personal success is rooted in the success of the people who work for you. This is a difficult adjustment to make, particularly if you are accustomed to being a top individual contributor where the feedback is more noticeable and more immediate. Slow feedback is further exacerbated by the tendency of management (in general) to be quick to identify problems, and slow to recognize good work. It may be years before someone compliments you on your skill as a manager, your low turnover rate, and the remarkable success of your people. Don't hold your breath, but eventually it will come. I recently had dinner with a group of people that had worked for me at a couple jobs. We reached the end of the dinner and they were asking me about my job prospects and where I was planning to go. One of them said, "You know, we're just waiting for you to get a good job so we can all come work for you again." That's the highest compliment I've received in my 20 or so years of management – and I wasn't even paying for dinner!

You probably don't want to wait 20 years to be complimented on your work. What can be done to help yourself recognize your achievements and keep on track with your plans? Set your expectations. Think in terms of what you want to see from your team as a whole in the next six months. Now think about what you want to see from each individual in your team in the next 6-12 months. Now you have goals and you can assess your progress quarterly and adjust as needed. If you don't set goals you can monitor, you will be consumed in the daily hassles of the job and forget to note what you've accomplished. If you need periodic reinforcement that you're doing a good job, take a look around you. Are your people happy and productive? Is your department doing the best it can to meet the company goals?

Nice Work!

Don't wait for someone to tell you you're doing a good job – you could grow very old. Instead, be sure you match your expectations to that of management. This will make your reviews considerably less painful. By aligning your goals with your management's goals, you can expect recognition on your accomplishments. It is important to review your goals with your management to be sure you agree. This calls attention to your interest in facilitating your manager's goals while subtly bringing his attention to the value you are bringing to the organization in meeting the goals he deems important.

Once you've cleverly aligned your goals with your manager's, be sure you allow that information to flow down to your team members. The individual goals within your group should be a subset of your goals that are a subset of your manager's goals that are a subset of the company goals. You will recognize contributions that help you meet your goals as will your manager.

Figure 19:
Goal Hierarchy

Don't forget to periodically review your goals and expectations and make any necessary adjustments. Stay flexible – your management's goals may change and you may need to change too. Stay realistic, or you will be disappointed and lose your motivation. Remember, your own job satisfaction will reflect down to your employees.

11 Growing Your Staff

What Do They Want to Be When They Grow Up?

Everyone in management will agree that training and development is an important part of the management job. Although there is a lot of lip service paid to this, how much of it actually occurs? Not nearly enough. As a good manager, it is vitally important to know where your people want to go, and to plan ways for them to get there. This will buy you loyalty, and will make people want to work for you. If you truly care about them, then you will truly care about their careers; both during the time they work for you, and when they pass beyond your company and seek their fortunes elsewhere.

Creating Opportunities

It is your job as a manager to create learning opportunities. Always plan training time into the project schedules. Not only is this realistic, but it also helps you to remember this constant need to develop your staff's skills. People in the technical industry need to show higher and higher skill levels. Be sure your people understand that you are aware of this, and that you care about their careers. Even though they may leave you eventually, training is an investment and not an expense. People will be loyal to you if you invest in their future, and you get to use the knowledge they gain while they work for you.

Who should you train? People who want to learn. If you have a severely limited budget, you want to be sure to train people who will be able to train other people. You also want to be sure you are training people who will be able to use their new knowledge in the near future, or the training will be lost. Invest your training dollars in people who want to learn and who can apply their knowledge.

Training can be a source of jealousy

This can be a source of jealousy within a department. Training opportunities are looked on as career opportunities, and in this industry, everyone has an eye toward their personal marketability. Keep that in mind, but also be sure you are using the company's training money intelligently and for the benefit of the company. Certification programs can be very valuable, if your company needs to utilize the skills that will be learned in the program. You don't want to spend your money on improving your employee's resumes without getting to use the skills for which you've paid.

While you want to train your most senior people and those who are the most eager to learn, remember you also need to spread the opportunities around. Ultimately, you want to get the most for your training dollars and give each person a chance to learn. Budget and time constraints may not allow this, and sometimes you may have a training plan that spans several years to get the desired training to those who want and deserve it.

On-Site or Off-Site?

Selecting on-site or off-site training depends on the type of class and the number of attendees. On-site training is good when large numbers need to be trained on the same topic. You do need to consider if you can afford to have that many people gone from their jobs during the training hours. Can you count on your people to do their jobs during lunch and after class? Generally, people are willing to do this. Is it possible to train fewer people? Should you be training a trainer who can teach the rest of your people?

I had a group that realized test automation was going to become a critical skill in the near future. Unfortunately, we had no money for formal training courses. Their solution? They coerced two coworkers who were experienced test automation engineers to conduct classes during lunchtime. The payment? Food, of course. The trainers got to eat for free, and the students quickly learned what they needed to know to be effective in our automation environment.

Off-site training is good for small numbers of people. It is almost a reward – a mini-vacation from the regular work at the office. It can also be a team-building exercise to send your group off together to a conference. Off-site training aids concentration, and allows more attention to be devoted to learning. There are few interruptions during off-site training, assuming the cell phones and Blackberries are turned off.

What about OJT?

On the Job Training (OJT) is still the most common training method, so recognize and facilitate it. Give your people time to work with new technologies. Give them access to mentors. Get them involved in the project as early as possible – it is easiest to learn while others are learning too. Build some extra time into the schedule for training, both for the trainers and the trainees.

When you are selecting seminars or conferences, be sure to look for practical application to your projects. While learning about testing in the object-oriented environment is interesting, it's probably not of much immediate use to your mainframe people. Be sure your company will see immediate benefits from these training sessions. If you cannot attend, be sure to debrief those who did, to see what they learned and how they can apply it. If you don't take the time to do the debriefing, they will quickly be consumed by the daily crises, and may not get a chance to implement and share their new knowledge.

Does Cross-Training Matter?

Cross-training is vitally important to your survival as a manager. People will stubbornly insist on going on vacation, having babies, and even changing jobs. Your only defense against this dynamic environment is to be sure that no one person is the only one who can perform a given task. Cross-training has to be enforced, or it won't happen. Only the very curious will seek out new tasks just for the sake of learning something. People tend to horde knowledge because it makes them more important and more sought-after. The only way to combat these tendencies is to implement a cross training plan and make it a part of everyone's review. Each person on your team should have a trainer and trainee assignment for each review period, and they should know that they will be evaluated on it. This will help them to take this responsibility seriously and make time for the tasks. It will also remind you to budget the time. Someone who is less experienced at a task may be slower than an experienced person. True, but better to spend the time now when they have someone to learn from than to wait until the guy with all the secrets walks out the door.

Cross-training isn't a luxury; it's a requirement

And what about automation? This has provided an excellent growth path for the QA Engineer who wants to do programming and design work. Automation is the technical path for the technically inclined and has now become a recognized specialty. It allows the application of design and programming skills within the QA environment and creates an opportunity to learn and apply the latest programming concepts. Automation is not for everyone, but for those with the skills and desire, it can be an excellent path for career growth.

Tracking the Strategy

So how can you create and implement a strategy for career growth? First, you have to talk to each individual about their plans and ambitions. This is an excellent topic for your initial employee meeting and a major discussion item for each annual review. Where do your people want to go? Map out the skills they have and the skills they want to the skills you need and can use. Make a spreadsheet of skills and a timetable. Once you know what's needed and wanted and when, you can begin planning how to do the training. If you envision needing 1-2 people with VB skills, maybe the best training alternative would be for those individuals to take a course at a local community college. If you have 15 people who need to lean OO technologies, terminology, and testing, maybe bringing in a trainer is your best bet.

Be sure to keep track of the individuals and their skills. You can use a mapping like this to set goals for skill advancement. It is also a great help when assigning people to project schedules. The following is an example of a mapping for skill sets:

Figure 20:

Skills Chart

	Visual Basic	Scripting	WinRunner Script	WinRunner Architecture	Test Case Design	Test Plan Design	Unix SysAdmin	Windows SysAdmin	Lotus Notes
Tom	E	E	W	W	E	E			
Fred			B	B	E	E	B		W
Tina	E	E	E	W	E	E		W	
Larry	B	B			E	B			
Diane							E	E	W
Naresh			W	W					
Bob	E	E	E	E	E		W		

E = Experienced
B = Beginner
W = Wants to learn

As with most management responsibilities, training requires planning. In order to know who to train, you need to know who already knows what. Can they teach others via cross-training or a more formal training program? Who needs to go to seminars and classes? How many can you afford to send? All these questions have to be answered at least annually when you create your training plan for the year (you do have one, right?). Charts like the one above help you track where people are, and where they want to be. Training is an investment. Use it wisely.

12 Delousing the Perfect Beast

Despite all our careful planning, intelligent hiring, and attention to career paths, sometimes there is a need to remove people from the group. One of the worst cases of this is when you have a person in a leadership position who isn't working out. In this section we'll discuss how to deal with those situations. We'll also look at what to do if you're having retention problems, and conversely, how to conduct a layoff without starting an exodus. Because firing someone is as much a responsibility for managers as initially hiring the right people, we'll look at how to do it as painlessly as possible. Just to round out this section, we'll also talk about how to handle a mass layoff or a bankruptcy. Sounds like it will be fun, doesn't it?

A Good Leader Gone Bad?

Finding good leaders is extremely difficult. Have you ever worked for a bad manager? If you've worked at more than a couple jobs, chances are you have. Maybe the better question is, have you ever worked for a good manager? Leadership requires a number of different qualities, and the combination of technical competence and people skills is unusual. True leaders really care about their people, and make it obvious in everything they do. They don't agree to unrealistic schedules without a fight; they don't agree to have their people work all night and through the weekend; they plan ahead for where their people will be in six months, one year, and two years. True leaders will be willingly followed. In this book, we've talked a lot about the qualities that make a good leader and skills and practices that will help you to be the best leader you can. Unfortunately, not everyone is able or willing to adopt these skills.

When you promote someone to a lead position or hire them from the outside, you are taking a risk that they won't have or won't be able to utilize the skills needed to be successful. Despite all your care and diligence, sometimes you have someone who you thought would be a good leader who just isn't. The good leader gone bad. What do you do?

A bad leader represents not just one problem, but two. The leader must be dealt with, and the people working for the bad leader are suffering until you fix the problem. You are responsible for the leader's people; don't shirk your duties. Because you have other people involved, you don't have as much time to spend observing the problem as you would if this were an individual contributor. First you have to determine the root cause of the problem, then decide if the situation is salvageable, and finally take whatever action is necessary.

Finding the Root Cause

Did you cause your lead to fail? What is the root cause of the leader's problem? Have you given them too much technical work and not allowed enough time for their management responsibilities? If this is the case, you should be able to fix the situation by helping out or reassigning some of the technical work. You do need to be aware that the person may be spending a disproportionate amount of time on the technical aspects of the job because that's where they are more comfortable. If you suspect this is the case, sit down with your lead and set out a daily schedule that allows time for administrative tasks. This will help call their attention to the other important aspects of their job and will give you a picture of how their time is currently allocated and why. Work with this person to help spread their time across all their responsibilities.

Are there too many personnel issues for this person to deal with in the time available? Giving your new lead the department's problem person isn't fair. Have you saddled your lead with too many personnel challenges? Remember, a problem person takes about 30% of an experienced leader's time. If you have unwittingly burdened your person with problem people, you probably need to look at reassigning personnel to give your lead a fair chance at the new job. Personnel problems are rarely easy to handle, and loading that on top of a lead who is trying to learn their way in a new position is really an unrealistic expectation.

Does this person have too much ego for the job? We had a joke at one company that the offices should be triangular, with the point down. That way there would be adequate space for the big heads of management. Funny, but too true. Some people don't appear to have an ego problem until you promote them. If they show up on Monday after the promotion with a changed appearance and an attitude of superiority, look out! Not only is this going to annoy you, but their people who were their peers on

Friday are going to resent this sudden change. People are highly sensitive to the appearance of a caste system. It is up to you to counsel your lead not to make sudden changes that will send the message that they are now superior to their former peers. Authority has to be earned before it will be respected.

Is your lead or manager creating more problems than they are solving? Is this just a short-term issue during the adjustment period? If not, you need to look at the problems they are creating, figure out what is behind them, and work with the person to stop the behaviors that are causing the problems. For example, if you find you now have their people in your office double-checking about task assignments, something is going wrong. Your lead should have enough credibility that the assignments they give are accepted straight away. In this instance, ask people why they feel they need to check with you. Were the assignments not clear? Was there not enough explanation given about the priority of the assignment? Do they just not trust the lead to be giving direction? Have you unconsciously undermined your own lead? Once you have your data, discuss it with the lead to get the problems addressed and fixed. Be careful though. You don't want the lead to feel that their people are against them and that you are siding with their people. This perceived ostracism will likely cause the lead to become defensive. It is vitally important that you be allied with your lead and that they understand you are working together as a management team.

A Puzzle of Problems

As you go along asking yourself each of these questions about one of your leads, remember that there are likely several things that are causing problems. Be sure you understand the scope of the issues before you make your action plan. It may be possible that the lead just needs more training either in management or in technical skills. There are cases where you have someone who is good with people, but too weak technically to gain their respect. In that case, training is likely your easy solution. If your lead is lacking in management skills, formal management training may be an option. A better solution is if you can mentor the person yourself. That way you can tailor the training to the person's needs and to your particular environment. This will only work if the person will listen to you. If there has already been some alienation between the two of you, consider getting

Usually, there is more than one issue

another manager who could be the person's advisor and confidant. If you can find a mentor for the person, be sure you don't interfere with the relationship. Everyone needs someone to whom they can confide their worries and shortcomings. If your lead doesn't have a good relationship with you, let them build one with another good manager.

Is your lead salvageable? This is one of the most important questions to answer correctly. If the lead is salvageable in a relatively short period of time, leave their people where they are. This will do the most for maintaining the confidence of the lead, and it is a public statement that you believe they can do the job. As soon as you start removing people out from under someone, you are publicly stating that you don't think they can lead those people. However, sometimes reassignments are required. Are there only a few individuals who are having conflicts with the lead? Can you move them to another lead without sending a premature negative message about the lead? You also want to look at whether these are junior or senior people who are having the problems. If your senior people are having issues and they are not normally complainers, meet with them and see if they have any suggestions. Make it clear that you are willing to listen and want to fix the problem, but be careful not to talk negatively about your lead. Enlist their help with the project, not the person.

Are Other Groups Affected?

You said WHAT?!? You also need to determine if damage has been done with relations with other departments. It helps to seek the advice of other department managers. This lets them know you are aware of a potential problem, and that you want to fix it as quickly as possible. By enlisting their help as advisors, you can also request their help as mentors to your problem lead. Other managers are likely to be in meetings with your lead, and can tell you what has happened in discussions when you weren't there. If there is a pattern of defensive behavior in a particular project meeting, you need to go to those meetings. Try to correct incorrect behavior as soon as it becomes apparent to you. It's very difficult to say, "Hey, I heard you were being sarcastic with the development manager in the project meeting today." If you do this, the person knows they are being discussed and will immediately become defensive. Instead, wait until you see the problem behavior firsthand before trying to offer guidance.

I once had a lead working for me who would repeatedly get in arguments with a development manager during project meetings. And the arguments were silly, usually deteriorating into a debate about who had more years of experience. Anytime I went to the meetings this didn't happen. Since my lead was already defensive, particularly about any issues involving this development manager, I didn't want to have a discussion with him based on hearsay. My solution was to enlist the help of the project manager who regularly attended the meetings and had witnessed these debates. After the next occurrence, he took my lead aside and told him his behavior was counterproductive, and unless the behavior changed, he would have to ask that my lead be removed from the project. This had the desired effect, and my lead came to me and told me about the problem and asked that he not be removed from the project. That got the whole problem out in the open, and we were able to determine why he felt inadequate on the project. I was able to arrange some technical training to bring him up to the level of knowledge he needed to feel comfortable when dealing with the very technical development manager.

As a manager, you are responsible for your people and their actions. Once you have a problem person, particularly someone in a high exposure position, it is likely that the problem is visible outside your department. If you think it is, be sure to brief your management on the problem and your action plan. Start to document the observed problems in the event that you might need to use the last resort of termination. Be sure that you are attending any external meetings in which your person is representing your department if you have concerns about their representation. If the problem is not yet public, project management is probably not the issue. That's the good news. Unfortunately, if project management isn't the issue, personnel management probably is.

You are responsible for your people and their actions

Eeek! Do Something!

Once you've determined there is a problem, you need to take action. Talk first – assess where the person is. Do they know there's a problem? If so, you can work from that point. Put your emphasis on where they think the problem is. If you see additional issues, address those at the next meeting. Encourage them to work on the problems they see first, and ease them into the recognition that there are others. If the person doesn't think there are any problems, you really have a problem! Now is the time to explain clearly and factually what the issues are and provide specific examples of the problem behavior, how it is perceived, and the results of their actions. Sometimes you are dealing only with perceptions, but those are reality and the lead needs to understand that if their people perceive that they are indifferent it doesn't matter if they care down in their heart. They have to fix the perception.

Once you have had the preliminary meeting, create an action plan. Ask what you can do to help your person. Admit that you are likely a part of the problem. Maybe you made an error with a promotion or a hiring decision? Did you not offer sufficient training? Did you push the person before they were ready? If you approach the conversation by assuming shared responsibility, you create an environment in which it is easier to admit fault. Be sure to give them a chance to talk about what they might have done differently. Offer training and mentoring. The action plan discussion is where you will find out how willing the person is to change. This is also the time to explain that you will be monitoring their efforts. They'll figure it out anyway, or at least suspect it, so you might as well be honest. Also explain that you may be attending project meetings if there are project management issues. Project issues are the easiest ones to fix, so by addressing these first you can ensure some early success and reinforce that positive changes can be made.

Project problems are the easiest to fix – personnel problem are the hardest

Managers and leads have a lot of ties outside your department. It is important to keep all interested parties informed that an action plan is in place. HR and your manager need to know that people who work for this person may be complaining and that you are on top of the situation. You want your supervisor to hear about the problems from you first. It is also a good idea to check with HR to see if there are any specific concerns about dealing with performance issues at the manager or lead level.

You may need to consider removing personnel responsibilities. This will be an overt statement that you don't think the lead can manage people unless it is handled very carefully. Sometimes you can reduce the number of people, thereby making the group more manageable. It may be necessary to remove all administrative responsibilities if the lead has proven that they are incapable of making unbiased personnel decisions. This can be particularly important if reviews and promotion decisions will be happening in the near future. I once had to remove personnel responsibilities from a manager right before a large number of performance reviews were due. Guess who got to spend their nights and weekends doing the reviews.

You Can't Wait Forever

Set a time limit for the expected improvement. A problem with a person in a leadership position has to be dealt with quickly because of the high visibility and the risk of adversely affecting projects and people. If the person is qualified, you may want to give them the option of a lateral transfer to a technical position. If, after your discussions, you find that your problem person wasn't aware there were any issues, they may need some time to adjust to the barrage of negative input you've just given them. Sending them home for a week or so to think about what they want to do will give them time away from the office, and the feeling of being under the microscope while they sort out what they want to do. It is a chance to do some career evaluation outside the demands of the work environment. It also allows you to gather more information. Remember to get input on what the person does well in addition to what they need to improve.

Set a realistic schedule for visible improvement. Give the person time to make changes, but you also can't be overly demanding on the patience of the lead's subordinates. There is usually an expectation of immediate action once problems have been raised with you. While this isn't realistic, you do have to be aware that there are a number of people waiting for you do to something about their problem. Be sure to get agreement with the person about the action plan and the timeframe. Once you have that agreement, document it and give a copy to the person so they understand that this is a serious undertaking, and that you are expecting them to accomplish the goals you have established.

One of the most important tasks to complete in any performance improvement plan is the follow-up. Conduct regular progress evaluation meetings at pre-scheduled intervals. Daily may not be too frequent if the problem is serious and you need it to be remedied quickly. Keep careful records of each meeting, and provide your employee with a copy of those records. Written documentation reinforces the seriousness of the process.

Be sure you are giving the person an honest chance. You have a lot invested in your leads, and you want them to succeed. Concentrate on helping to solve the problem, and don't be swayed by whatever griping may be occurring in the background. Give the person time to improve with a realistic plan with assessable milestones. It's important that progress can be charted along the way since the proposed improvements may seem intimidating at the onset.

It's Not Working ...

And what if the improvement plan doesn't work? Sometimes it doesn't. A termination can be done by either party, but it is almost always better to let someone quit with their dignity intact than to fire them. Lots of excellent technical people try management positions only to decide it's not for them. There's nothing wrong with that. It is not necessarily a failure to try a career change and decide it's not for you. The real failure is to make the change and stay with it even though you're abominable in the new position. Once again, the lateral transfer out of management to technical may be just the solution.

If a termination is inevitable, gather your documentation together, consult with your supervisor and HR, and plan the termination. We'll discuss terminations in more depth in a later section. One important thing to remember when terminating a lead or manager is that other people will be watching, and it might reflect badly upon you if you put the person there in the first place. It pays to be sure you've exhausted all other options. Also, be sure that your organization is ready to cover the loss.

Oh No! Good People Are Leaving!

Sometimes, even in a stable company, people start leaving. As soon as one leaves, he tells his friends how great the new company is and suddenly everyone is updating their resumes. This phenomenon happens in cycles depending on the economy, the spawning of new companies, and the general restlessness of a group. When you find yourself in this situation, the first task is to determine why people are leaving. If you can identify the problem, see if you can fix it. Allow yourself to consider if they should be leaving. Should you be thinking about leaving also?

Not enough money?
Boring work?
Too much work?

How do you find out why people are leaving? Ask them! People who are leaving will be honest with you if they trust you. They have nothing to lose. Listen to the grapevine too. As soon as people start leaving, discussion will begin about the pros and cons of the company. You'll also find out where people are thinking of going and why. This gives you some fodder to mount a campaign to retain your people.

Is money the issue? If so, review the salaries as was discussed in previous chapters. If the salaries are unfair, lobby for long-term change. Since your problem is immediate, even though a long-term solution is the correct one, you also need to show a short-term change. Look at possible bonus or merit increase plans that you could implement immediately. When you are looking at merit increases, consider making them retroactive. If your salaries are fair, is there other compensation that is not competitive? Evaluate the stock and bonus plans. Look at the current reward system and see if improvements could be made. Honestly though, you may not have much power to change the salary scheme. Always try though, and be sure you convince your management to continue the fight by providing supporting data like competitor's salaries, counter-offers from other companies, etc.

We're Bored

Is the work an issue? This happened to me at one job. The pay was good and the environment was excellent, but the work was just plain boring. I had a terrible time retaining high-caliber people. What's the solution? Ferret out new, interesting projects and announce them to the group. Show there is hope for more interesting work. In my case, I started three separate automation projects, one of which was to build a hardware simulator. This kept my most talented people interested and involved. I also recruited some extra side projects from another division so we could have a break from the monotonous work that was our mainstay. You may also want to consider finding training courses for your people and getting them enrolled. By committing your resources to their training, you are making a statement that you believe there is a benefit to what they are learning and you are interested in developing their careers.

What if no interesting projects are coming? Start some. Think ahead about what you might need in the future to make the work more efficient. Again, automation projects are a good opportunity here to use people's minds, and to create something you need. Test tracking systems are also a good investment when you have some spare time. You can always look to buy a package and use your resources to perform the integration. Remember, you don't have to be able to dedicate a whole team full time to your new projects. Part time effort will suffice and will keep people interested while still allowing the main thrust of the work to be accomplished. People who are partially assigned to an interesting project will find the time to get it done.

Also consider starting some small development projects. Is there some software for which you could assume maintenance responsibilities? A small demo or proof-of-concept project that your people could help with? Could your group do some professional services-type customization? These are just some ideas that might work for you. The important thing to remember is to make the job more interesting for your folks while still getting the boring work done. Everyone is more productive if they like what they're doing, and they will work hard to get through their mundane tasks to get to the stuff they really want to do. Use ideas like this to keep people while producing products that were not on the schedule and not in the budget.

There's Too Much Work!

Are schedules the problem? Are people feeling overwhelmed and out of control? This happens frequently in small companies where extraordinary effort becomes the expectation. If this is a problem for your group, you need to look at how you are presenting the schedule information. Are your people able to see clearly what is coming? Are you explaining their new assignments and projects? Do they understand how important their contribution is to the success of the company? Can you show that the new projects will be interesting and will provide new learning opportunities?

Everyone needs to understand their contribution is important

Sometimes when people feel overwhelmed, it is because they don't feel they're accomplishing anything toward a goal. This is where tracking test case completion can be extremely helpful. If you run 10 test cases a day for a week and find no bugs, you may feel like you've accomplished nothing and could have called in sick (of work) and given the same benefit to the company (and worked on your tan too). If, on the other hand, you can see on a chart that successfully executing your 70 test cases resulted in 100 priority risks being mitigated, now you can see the benefits of your labors. People who are feeling overwhelmed, useless, or ineffective will tend to slack off and assume their job isn't important. As a manager or lead, your job is to be sure everyone understands the importance of their contribution.

One of the most difficult schedule situations I have encountered was when I was working for a company that was a division of a much larger company. We didn't control the schedules and had no view of what projects we would be working on three months in the future. This made planning very difficult, and it was hard to keep people motivated because they couldn't see where they were going and how their skills would be used. To make matters worse, there were perpetual rumors about projects being cancelled. The only successful method I found for dealing with this was to have a constant flow of background projects that people could depend on. I found them by scouring the company for non-scheduled work. Because they had the security of knowing there was always something to work on, they were much better able to handle the uncertainty of the production schedules.

What If You're the Problem?

Are you the problem? That's not good news. Value the person who had the guts to tell you! Now you have to figure out what you're doing wrong and fix it. Once you determine the errors of your ways, call a meeting to explain that you were wrong and explain what you will do to correct the situation. Be honest and act quickly.

I once had the displeasure of working for a manager who always criticized, never complimented. No matter what we did, it seemed that we should have done it sooner, better, or faster. It wore us down. And, being human, we concluded that since sacrificing our personal lives and working long hours wasn't satisfying our boss, we might as well work less hard and be in trouble anyway. The net result? Our boss was still unhappy and we felt guilty. In an exit interview, one of my soon-to-be-former coworkers told our boss about the problem. He was stunned. He thought he had been encouraging us to work harder. He'd had no idea about the demoralizing effect his constant "constructive" criticism had. He called a meeting and apologized, and asked us to please tell him if he did it again. What a difference! That division turned around in a day, all thanks to the guts of our exiting friend and the honesty of our boss.

Is the company the problem? If so, get some help from above. Ask your manager to address the group and discuss the issues. Identify key concerns and be sure they are addressed. You may also need to query HR and see what they know about the problems. They do the exit interviews, and they may be seeing a pattern.

If you request help from your supervisor, or higher, you may want to prime them before the meeting so they know which concerns are most prevalent. I once had a problem where people were leaving the company in droves, and my department was being severely affected. The main concern was that company sales were down, and people were worried about their jobs. As the developers left, QA was having to assume more responsibility, schedules were being missed, and morale was down. My vice president decided to give a pep talk to the QA group. The first slide he put up was titled "QA – An Exiting Place to Be!" So true. We think he meant to say "exciting" but we thoroughly enjoyed his typo. This one typographical error did a lot to restore morale and pull the group together. It became the group joke, and got us through the rough months ahead.

The Exodus Has Begun

An exodus tends to feed on itself

The more people leave, the more people will leave. Sad, but true. An exodus feeds on itself because people are forced to consider whether they should be leaving also. If you can, convince people that the outside world really isn't better. Find people who have left the company and returned. Use them as examples. I've found it helpful to pursue rumors of people who may have been ready to leave the company but decided to stay. You need some real data to back up your arguments of why people shouldn't be leaving.

Should people be leaving? For example, is there a severe layoff coming? Tell them what you know, within the limits of what you're allowed to disclose. Sometimes a constructive information leak can accomplish this without putting you into a bad position with your management. Your people need to be able to trust you. If you were in their position, is this information you would want or would need to have? Layoff rumors are probably the most difficult to handle. You want people to be able to start looking for a new job, but you don't want to risk sabotage. It depends on how well you know your people, and how large the risk is. I've never had one of my people sabotage a system, but I always double-check the backups when an announcement is eminent. I think I've probably been lucky with this since I've certainly heard a lot of credible horror stories. One big advantage to general knowledge of an upcoming layoff is those who were already planning to leave may volunteer for the layoff, thus saving someone else's job. In deciding how much information to disclose, you have to operate within your own comfort level with the situation. Your management will determine how much information can be disclosed, and when. Be sure you follow the rules, or you may be putting your own job on the line.

That's it! I quit!

What if you're leaving? Sometime in your career, you will have to face this difficult situation. You've carefully built and developed your group, but now it is time for you to go pursue another job. It is critically important to be able to honestly explain to your group why you are leaving. If you are leaving for personal reasons (unrelated to the company), this is easy. If you are leaving because you feel the company is not a good place to work, you need to be very careful to handle the situation professionally. You owe it to the company to keep your people in place once you depart, and to provide the easiest possibly transition to the next management. But people aren't stupid. Be honest. They won't believe rhetoric, and will lose respect for you if you attempt to purport it.

Before you make any announcements, talk to your supervisor and see how they'd like you to handle it. Get an action plan in place for who will take over your group. Be sure everything is determined before the announcement occurs. People are basically selfish, and their first concern will be how this change will affect them. Be ready to answer their questions and calm their fears. Telling your managers and leads first is usually a good idea. They will have to do the damage control, so give them the information and a chance to absorb it. If they've been close to you and you have been their mentor, they need some time to adapt to the changes.

When it comes time to make the announcement, I'm most comfortable telling the group myself. Tell the truth, and give them the reasons for your decision. People may sometimes need to use you as a reference, so be sure to give them your contact information. It is also good if you can explain how the transition will be handled to the new management. If your supervisor can be there too, it will provide the message of continuity, which will put more fears to rest.

Quitting and leaving a department you have built is one of the most difficult things you'll do in your career. Be sure you handle it professionally and honestly. You will meet those people again in later jobs – bet on it.

Terminations – Getting the Job Done as Painlessly as Possible

If someone has reached the point where you need to fire them, they deserve it. Whereas I think layoffs are one of the most difficult things to do as a manager, firing is much easier. You do have to put serious diligence into gathering your data together, and ending someone's job is certainly never a decision to be made lightly. Once you have the data gathered, the conclusion is obvious.

You should assume the process to terminate someone will take about 90 days. It varies between companies, but on an average this is about right. That means you can't use firing as the easy way out. It is truly the last resort for an unrecoverable situation. As you are gathering your data to do the termination, reflect on why you need to fire this person. Was it a hiring error? Was there a training issue? Sometimes a person is under-skilled for a job and there isn't enough time to teach them the skills they will need. Sometimes they just can't learn the skills they need to advance with the technology required for the job. Whatever the reason, you need to understand what you did wrong with this person that led to such an ignominious end so you don't repeat your mistake.

I once hired a guy with an excellent internal reference who didn't work out. During the interview process, I asked him if the commute would be an issue since he lived about two hours from the job site. He explained that he was planning to get a divorce and would be relocating to an apartment closer to work. OK. He was well-qualified for the job, and one of my people had worked with him at a previous company and thought highly of him. I hired him. It quickly became apparent that all he did each day was stare at the wall in front of his monitor. He wasn't able to pick up the new software, and wasn't able to build the automation cases for which he'd been hired. After several discussions regarding his performance, he finally told me that his divorce plans had been thwarted by the unexpected arrival of his in-laws. The in-laws were not just visiting but had moved in with him, and his wife had made it clear that divorce would not be acceptable. Poor guy. So not only was the commute burning him out, but his personal life was in shambles. Unfortunately, I had nothing with which to defend him. It wasn't like he had been a good and valuable employee and was going through some rough times so I could give him some leeway. He was brand new, and had done nothing to prove himself on the job. When I told him I'd have to terminate him due to lack of performance unless there was a radical change, he honestly told me that I would probably have to fire him because he just couldn't concentrate.

I gathered my documentation and terminated him with as much warning and counseling as I could supply. In retrospect, I don't know what I would have done differently. He interviewed well, he was qualified for the job, and I had excellent internal references. Sometimes you just can't predict performance.

When you have to fire someone, it helps to confide in a peer. For one thing, you need some moral support. Even though you are completely justified in your termination, as I was in the above example, it still isn't a happy event. By talking to a peer, you can sometimes get an independent view of your problem child and maybe some insight that will help you see the path to save this person. Hey, it might happen.

Planning the Termination or Plotting the Rehabilitation

Plan for one verbal review at the beginning, maybe several. In these sessions, provide concrete examples of unacceptable performance. Be sure your data is accurate. Explain your expectations, again with specific examples of what should have happened. Give a detailed schedule for your expectations and provide measurable milestones. It is important that you spend at least half the time in this session listening. You'll find out if the person perceives there is a problem, if they really want to change to meet your expectations, and if there is hope for salvage.

Creating measurable milestones for a QA team member is particularly difficult. You want to be sure to avoid a quota system. Some parts of the code will always have more bugs, and some bugs are more difficult to find. You can't say that the person isn't doing a good job because they only found 50 bugs in a piece of software. You can say they aren't doing a good job if someone else finds 100 bugs that should have been caught with the test cases planned for that section of the code. But you have to be very careful when comparing the performance of two people. Unless they are working in the same area and have the same general skill level, it's unfair to make a comparison. You may get no useful information out of comparing bug counts, time taken to complete tests, time to write test plans, etc. If you do decide to use comparison data, be very sure you are being fair. Not only is it the right thing to do, it may help you legally if litigation results from the termination.

Be sure your milestones are measurable and evaluation criteria are clear

Picking Performance Criteria

There are some areas that lend themselves as performance evaluation items. You can have two people with similar experience test the same software and compare the outcome. If you don't have two comparable people, or testing is too nebulous to use for evaluation, consider giving the person more measurable tasks. Test planning activities are good for this. Paperwork is tangible, and you can set realistic deadlines for completion. Automation projects require coding and can be tracked by milestones. These work well if you have a person who is technically capable of doing automation. This is also an area where you can afford to have someone not do a good job because it can be checked before it is implemented, unlike letting your low performer test a critical part of software that has to ship. Test scripting is also a good measurement for performance. Any level of tester should be able to write test scripts (step-by-step descriptions of what needs to be tested). While this may not be the most interesting work, it is easy to assess for quality and completeness.

When you have determined and agreed on the evaluation criteria, set the schedule for the next evaluation. Allow enough time for the person's performance to improve, yet limit the time so the disease doesn't spread. If you have a poor performer you have to carefully balance giving them enough time to correct their problems, and acting promptly to remove the problem. It is important to get them to agree to the evaluation criteria and the method of determining if they have met the criteria. Be sure you set the bar such that they will have to perform to achieve the goals. If you make the standards too low, they'll meet the criteria without actually putting in any effort to improve their performance and you will have to extend the evaluation period.

Document each meeting you have with the person, and provide them with a copy of your notes. At the end of the allotted period, you need to evaluate their progress. If they have made a drastic improvement in their performance, you're finished with this phase. Continue to monitor their performance closely to ensure they don't slip back into their old ways. Keep on providing detailed feedback for several more months – both so they know you're still watching them, and to reinforce that their performance is important to the success of the group and the company. If, on the other hand, they have failed to meet the agreed criteria, you need to move to the next step in the process.

Put It in Writing

Up to now the discussions have been relatively informal. If this has not worked, it's time to formalize the proceedings. As with the verbal steps, you again review the performance, create the evaluation milestones, and get the employee's agreement. This time though, you formally document the procedure and provide a copy to your supervisor and HR. When you present the written documentation of the meeting, emphasize the seriousness of the issues and make it clear that this is now a formal procedure.

Once again, you're in the monitoring phase. When the time period ends, do the evaluation again. If this formal phase worked, you will need to continue to monitor performance and provide feedback for the next six months or so. Watch this person closely since the verbal reprimand didn't work. Did they not believe you were serious before? Did you set the same type of criteria in the written reprimand as in the verbal? If this formal phase didn't help, go on to the next step.

The End

Terminations are handled differently in each company. Have a discussion with your HR department and your supervisor regarding how the situation should be handled. Clarify all the events with HR. Who walks the person out? Who cuts the network access? Do you have to pack their office for them? Should there be another manager or HR representative present at the termination?

Be sure you're in a defensible legal position

When you have all your paperwork ready and all the details worked out, conduct the termination. I prefer to have someone else present; either another manager, or HR. This helps prevent any misinterpretation or misrepresentation of what occurred. State the issues clearly and objectively. This is not the time for discussion; they've already heard this information before and had their chance to correct their performance. It is too late for promises and second tries at this point. This session is simply a statement of the facts. State unemotionally that their job is terminated. Explain what termination means in terms of benefits, etc. Give them an HR contact to call once the news has been absorbed. Sometimes the person will be routed to HR to finish out the details. If so, escort them to HR yourself. You'll feel much better on the return trip.

Layoffs without Exodus

Layoffs are inevitable in the software industry. Some companies are more immune to it than others, but it is more than likely that you will someday have to conduct a layoff. As I said earlier, to me conducting a layoff is the absolute worst management task. Unfortunately, I've had to do it several times. As much as I hate to dwell on it, it is best to be prepared.

Planning the Layoff

Depending on your position within the company, you may be involved in a series of planning meetings during which the scope of the layoff will be determined. These meetings can be very difficult and sometimes erupt into a turf war where groups are intent on retaining their headcount at the cost of decimating other groups. Your job in these meetings is to be factual, and to keep your emotions in check. Explain your workload, and how various layoff proportions will affect your ability to meet schedules and maintain quality. You will want to be sure that the layoff is a fair reduction based on workload. If the layoff will result in projects being cut, terminating the entire project team may not be the most efficient way to achieve the reduction. You will want to look at the skills within that project team, and the skills elsewhere in the department to determine the best method of meeting the reduction goals.

In some cases, the layoff will be unfairly loaded against QA. It is unfortunate, but unless you have been successful in creating the awareness of the importance of QA, your management may decide that decimating your department has fewer long-term consequences than eliminating development personnel who are busily creating the next generation product. If you find yourself in this situation, this should compel you to begin establishing that awareness for the future. For now, though, you have to deal with the situation at hand. It is usually the assumption in a layoff that the reduction is temporary and eventually the staff will build up again. If this is the case, state your case with factual information regarding the training and replacement times for your personnel. Explain the workload and workforce allocation, as this is probably not known outside your immediate department. Discuss the risk analysis basis of testing and the risk mitigation your department performs. This will help everyone see the costs of eliminating certain personnel. Finally, explain the total schedule impact. This should be done in terms of risk management and date slippage.

Once the layoff proportions are determined (fairly we hope), gather the information you'll need to present the facts of the layoff to your group. Will other departments be affected? You don't have to agree with the reasons for the layoff or the way it will occur, but you do need to understand what's happening so you can explain it to your people, some of whom are personally affected.

Picking the Victims

What is management's goal in this layoff? Are they trying to reduce payroll? Reduce headcount? Are pay cuts an option? Could some employees convert to contractors and save the overhead costs? Once you get this information, give yourself some time to digest it. How can you best meet management's goals and still have an effective department?

Do I finally get to use my layoff list??

Every manager has a list of people they would like to get rid of. And here you are presented with the need to reduce headcount. It's a perfect situation, right? Wrong. Unfortunately, layoffs have their own legalities to consider. In some states, you can't lay off someone because of job performance, but only if their job is being eliminated. If you're doing a large layoff, this is a significant consideration. You can't rehire to those same positions for some period of time – often as long as six months. Now whom can you do without? You may have a poor performer in a key position. Are they better than nothing? That may be your only option. You want to be sure you are always in a defensible position. If you are unsure and your HR group can't clarify for you, ask to talk to your company's attorney about your liability. In some states, you can be personally sued (as well as the company).

Now that your mind is clouded with the legalities of the situation, determine whom you want to and need to lay off. Match that list against those you can legally lay off. With any luck, there are some overlaps. Make your layoff list accordingly from the union of the two lists. Be sure to watch out for protected groups (over 40, etc.). Again, check with HR or legal counsel so you stay within the safe parameters. If you have managers working for you, you want to include them in this decision process, assuming you are allowed to tell them. I've been in situations where managers were going to be laid off alongside their teams.

Doing the Dirty Deed

There is no good way to conduct a layoff, although companies continue to invent new and creative ways. The best method is to do it as quickly as possible, removing those who have been laid off and getting everybody else calmed down and back to work as soon as possible. You may choose to do the layoffs individually, picking your victims out of the herd one at a time. This creates a terrible aura while the layoffs are occurring. Everyone waits to see if they'll be the next one called. You can feel a kinship with the prairie dog colony as the hawk circles. While you want to consider the feelings of those being terminated, your prime concern is to not damage the remaining group. Assure them they are safe as soon as you can.

When you deliver the message to those being laid off, be compassionate, factual, and concise. State why they are being laid off, the scope of the layoff, and offer any help you can provide. Offer your contact information as a reference if you can do so. Reassure them that it is not a job performance issue or a personal issue, but rather a business decision. Be sincere, be concerned, and be honest, but get it done quickly.

If there are outplacement agencies available to help with the layoff, they can be a big help. They will take over the newly-terminated people and handle all the details, allowing you to get back to those you are keeping. Outplacement agencies are great at getting people started looking for their next jobs and providing services to assist in creating resumes, finding potential employers, and improving job skills.

Don't underestimate the shock of a layoff

Once the dirty deed is done, get back to your remaining people. Explain what was done and why. Tell them what the severance package was, as that will reassure them that the company isn't completely heartless. Tell them who was laid off – don't make them check the phone list to figure it out. Tell them how other departments were affected. Since everyone is now concerned about their job security, give whatever assurances you can that this won't happen again.

I worked at one company that did a major layoff by removing 1-2 people each day over the period of several months. We made a program that would compare the phone list day to day to see who was no longer with us. Talk about a demoralizing environment!

A layoff is a big shock to an organization – don't underestimate it. It shakes people's security and makes them wonder if they should seek another job. In a bad job market this is particularly difficult because people aren't certain that they will easily be able to go elsewhere. Give people time to adjust to the change, and to the resulting insecurity. It is usually good to have another meeting a couple days after the layoff to field questions, and get people talking about it openly. Answer the questions honestly, and if you don't know the answer, find someone who does. After one significant layoff, I had a meeting with my people. They had several questions regarding long-term business plans. Since I didn't feel qualified to answer their questions, I requested the president of the company to come and meet with them. He did so, and it was a beneficial meeting all around.

Once the questions have been answered, calm the waters and get everyone back to work. The best way to do this is to start discussions and meetings about future projects. This gets their minds back on their jobs and their future work. Also be cognizant that these people have friends who are now out of work. Don't plan a big party to raise morale; that will only incense people because money is being spent on parties when their friends no longer have jobs.

Bankruptcy and Mass Layoffs

Can you tell I worked for a .com?

You may wonder why you care since your job is now gone too. Because you're a professional, that's why. Even in the face of a company shutdown or a huge layoff, people will still look to you for guidance. You're likely to hire some of these people again in your next job, so stay in touch. Get that contact list together and keep it current. Your former employees are going to need you for references, so be sure they have a way to get in touch with you while you are also on the job search road. Because you are still considered their leader, people will want to talk to you and do some grieving about their former job. Let them. They need to talk. Plan your reunion lunches now, so you can keep the ties in place. This is a great way to build your network of allies across many companies.

13 Admiring Our Perfect Beast

This book has followed our perfect beast from the time it was born, to when it was fed, raised and developed, vaccinated, and buried. We've learned how to mold this beast into the best working whole it can be, recognizing that the difficulties which drive us crazy as managers are often just what it needs to become stronger. We've also learned that the people who compose our beast spend the majority of their non-sleeping time at work. At least we hope the beast hasn't been sleeping at work! If it has, go back to the vaccination section! With all that time spent at work, our job as managers is to ensure that it has been used as profitably as possible for the whole beast. In fact, this is what management is all about.

Don't get distracted from the long-term goals by short-term project crises and silly meetings; your job is to create a mutually beneficial relationship where your company, your individual contributors, and your management team get the most possible from the employment relationship. Everyone wants to look forward to coming to work in the morning (except for the people with night jobs, of course). People spend a significant number of hours each workday involved in work activities. Remember that this is a big chunk out of someone's life. The time they spend at work must be meaningful to them or they won't stay with it.

Your job is to create a mutually beneficial relationship

Let's recap. What are the critical components of job satisfaction? There are several, and the value assigned to each component varies with each person over time. The three main factors are the following:

- Monetary rewards must be adequate. A person can't stay at a job (even if they love it) if it does not provide enough money to pay the bills.
- Intellectual stimulation must be sufficient. Some people don't need much, others do. The happiest people will be interested in what they're doing. Those who are being challenged will bring their best to the job.
- A good working environment must exist. Again, this is a matter of what makes a good working environment for each person. Some people care if they get free specialty coffee. Others are only concerned that there be

sufficient air conditioning to keep the computers from frying. To each his own. In general, you want an environment where all the "important" needs are met, and where people are comfortable.

Each employee's job satisfaction is critical to your success. You will only be as successful as your people can make you, and your success is determined by how well your group functions toward meeting the company's goals. Your contribution is now measured in how well your people are working, and that is determined by your ability to hire, manage, and keep good employees.

Since good, effective, able, and willing employees are the key to our success as managers, how do we find them and keep them? As we've discussed in this book, we have to look at our employees as people and seek to develop them in their careers. What are the critical factors in accomplishing this?

- **Interview carefully.** The job is a whole lot easier when you start with the very best people in the first place. We talked about interviewing tips: questions to ask, and warning signs to observe. Honing your skills as an interviewer is one of the surest ways to guarantee your success as a manager.

- **Care.** You have to care about your employees. They can tell if you do or not. If you honestly can't find it in your heart to care about your subordinates as people, you're in the wrong career. You may be able to get people to grudgingly work for you, but that will be it. You won't be able to get top performance, and they'll be the first ones to run for the door at any sign of a downturn or a better offer.

- **Be consistent.** Define the working environment for your people and their interaction with you, and stick with it. Don't be a flake – no one wants to work for a flake.

- **Be honest.** Make your people feel secure in dealing with you. Build trust.

- **Know what you're doing technically.** Earn their respect in their arena. Stay current with the technology your company is using. Take some classes if necessary. You have to be able to speak intelligently in meetings with other technical people. You may need to provide technical guidance to your group – or at least you need to know enough to hire someone who can.

- **Correct your mistakes**. You're going to make mistakes. Be honest when you do. If your mistakes are in the hiring area, counsel when you can and fire when you must. Act promptly and decisively once you have gathered your information.

- **Don't forget things**. Like the old Federal Express commercial that said they handled every package as if it were their most important one because they never knew which one was the most important. Don't forget things people tell you. Their vacation request might be critical to them, even if it seems unimportant to you at the time. If you find that people frequently send you mail confirming what you've discussed with them, look out. They probably think you're forgetting or misremembering what transpired. Assume that anything brought to you is important to someone, and treat it accordingly.

- **Be yourself**. It's the one thing you can do consistently and honestly. You have enough on your mind already. Keeping up a façade of being someone you're not will exhaust you, and it won't work in the long run anyway.

This book has covered a lot of management topics, particularly those unique to managing in the technical world. Management is basically common sense and treating people the way you'd like to be treated. Even the best managers need to be reminded that there are real people working for them – people with hopes and dreams. It is the people who will make your group succeed. People have troubles; some stemming from work, some from home. But by creating a productive working environment, you can get the best from your employees and give them a job in which they are comfortable to make the best contribution they possibly can. This is, after all, the goal. We're trying to make people happy and interested in their jobs so they can do great work and benefit the company, as well as themselves.

Management can be the most rewarding of careers. Take advantage of the opportunity you've been given, and create that world-class organization. Stay on the right path by frequently asking yourself, "Am I being honest? Am I being consistent? Would I want to work for me?" If you can apply the skills discussed in this book and use your power wisely, you will indeed be able to build and maintain that elusive organization that is effective and happy: the perfect beast.

Bibliography

Beizer, Boris. *Software Testing Techniques*. New York, NY: Van Nostrand Reinhold, 1990. There is a discussion in this book about the attributes of a good tester.

Black, Rex. *Critical Testing Processes: Plan, Prepare, Perform, Perfect*. Boston, MA: Addison-Wesley Professional, 2003. Takes a good look at the processes you need and, maybe more importantly, the ones you don't.

————. *Managing the Testing Process: Practical Tools and Techniques for Managing Hardware and Software Testing*. New York, NY: Wiley, 2002. Includes a discussion about creating a skills matrix, organizing the test group within the overall organization, and includes some pointers on contracting and outsourcing.

Craig, Rick D. *Systematic Software Testing*. Boston, MA: Artech House Publishers, 2002. Good discussions regarding effective leadership and building respect.

DeMarco, Tom. *Slack: Getting Past Burnout, Busywork, and the Myth of Total Efficiency*. New York, NY: Broadway Books, 2001. Includes discussions regarding organizations that have downsized the creativity out of themselves by eliminating middle management and making everyone tactical – no eye to strategy.

DeMarco, Tom and Timothy Lister. *Peopleware: Productive Projects and Teams*. New York, NY: Dorset House Publishing, 1999. Includes great case studies, and good discussions about delivering bad news and about meetings.

Drucker, Peter. *The Essential Drucker: The Best of Sixty Years of Peter Drucker's Essential Writings on Management*. New York, NY: Collins, 2003. This title is always a good general reference.

Ensworth, Patricia. *The Accidental Project Manager: Surviving the Transition from Techie to Manager*. New York, NY: Wiley, 2001. This book talks about landing in the job whether you wanted it or not, recognizing your job is no longer what it used to be – now it's managing rather than doing. It also discusses conducting performance reviews and dealing with problem employees.

Graham, Dorothy, Erick van Veenendaal, Isabel Evans, and Rex Black. *Foundations of Software Testing: ISTQB Certification.* London, UK: International Thomson Business Press, 2006. This book is based on the ISTQB foundation syllabus and provides a good overall view of the software testing world.

ISTQB Foundation Syllabus (management). www.istqb.org. A great summary of an international approach to unifying the software testing community.

Jones, Capers. *Software Assessments, Benchmarks, and Best Practices.* Boston, MA: Addison-Wesley Professional, 2000. This includes an interesting discussion regarding defect removal effectiveness.

Koomen, Tim and Martin Pol. *Test Process Improvement.* Harlow, England; Reading, MA: Addison-Wesley Professional, 1999.

Pol, Martin and Erik Van Veenendaal. *Software Testing: A Guide to the Tmap™ Approach.* Boston, MA: Addison-Wesley Professional, 2001.

Rothman, Johanna. *Hiring the Best Knowledge Workers, Techies & Nerds: The Secrets and Science of Hiring Technical People.* New York, NY: Dorset House Publishing Company, 2004.

Spillner, Andreas, Tilo Linz and Hans Schaeffer. *Software Testing Foundations: A Study Guide for the Certified Tester Exam.* 2nd ed. Santa Barbara, CA: Rocky Nook, 2007. This book is based on the ISTQB foundation syllabus and provides a good overall view of the software testing world.

Wysocki, Robert K., Ph.D. *Effective Project Management: Traditional, Adaptive, Extreme.* New York, NY: Wiley, 2006. This title provides good general project management information.

Yourdon, Edward. *Outsource: Competing in the Global Productivity Race.* Boston, MA: Prentice Hall, 2004. This title provides a good view of the pros and cons of outsourcing.

Check with your HR department! – for information on reviews and merit increases that are particular to your company.

Index